THE
COLLIE

BY ANNA KATHERINE NICHOLAS

Title page photo: Four generations in a family of Collies. *Far left,* Ch. Azalea Hill's Court Jester at age seven years. *Next,* his son Ch. Azalea Hill's Strike Force at two years of age. *Bottom,* Strike Force's son, Azalea Hill's Marksman, age three months. *Far right,* Ch. Azalea Hill's Shawn, ten-year-old bitch, whose sire was litter sister to Jester's sire. Owned by Mrs. Richmond Fairbanks, Greenville, South Carolina. Photo by Frank Pearce, Greenville News-Piedmont.

t.f.h.

© 1986 by T.F.H. Publications, Inc. Ltd.

Distributed in the UNITED STATES by T.F.H. Publications, Inc., 211 West Sylvania Avenue, Neptune City, NJ 07753; in CANADA by H & L Pet Supplies Inc., 27 Kingston Crescent, Kitchener, Ontario N2B 2T6; Rolf C. Hagen Ltd., 3225 Sartelon Street, Montreal 382 Quebec; in ENGLAND by T.F.H. Publications Limited, 4 Kier Park, Ascot, Berkshire SL5 7DS; in AUSTRALIA AND THE SOUTH PACIFIC by T.F.H. (Australia) Pty. Ltd., Box 149, Brookvale 2100 N.S.W., Australia; in NEW ZEALAND by Ross Haines & Son, Ltd., 18 Monmouth Street, Grey Lynn, Auckland 2 New Zealand; in SINGAPORE AND MALAYSIA by MPH Distributors (S) Pte., Ltd., 601 Sims Drive, # 03/07/21, Singapore 1438; in the PHILIPPINES by Bio-Research, 5 Lippay Street, San Lorenzo Village, Makati Rizal; in SOUTH AFRICA by Multipet Pty. Ltd., 30 Turners Avenue, Durban 4001. Published by T.F.H. Publications Inc. Manufactured in the United States of America by T.F.H. Publications, Inc.

Contents

About the Author

Since early childhood, Anna Katherine Nicholas has been involved with dogs. Her first pets were a Boston Terrier, an Airedale, and a German Shepherd. Then in 1925 came the first of the Pekingese, which breed she continued to own for more than thirty years. Now her home is shared with two Miniature Poodles and nine Beagles, some her own and the others belonging to Marcia Foy who lives with her.

Miss Nicholas is best known throughout the Dog Fancy as a writer and as a judge. Her first magazine article (about Pekingese) appeared in the original *"Dog News"* around 1930. It was followed by more than two decades as a Pekingese columnist, then during the next twenty years or so by articles geared to the general interest of all dog fanciers which have appeared in many leading magazines devoted to dogs. Currently she is a featured regular columnist for *Dog World, Kennel Review and Canine Chronicle.* Her *Dog World* column, "Here, There and Everywhere" was the Dog Writers Association of America winner of the Best Series in a Dog Magazine Award for 1979.

Miss Nicholas's first book, *The Pekingese*, was written at the request of the Judy Publishing Co. Two editions sold out completely, the first in the late 1930's, the second in the following decade. Next came *The Skye Terrier Book*, in the 1960's, published by the Skye Terrier Club of America. These books are now collector's items.

In 1970 Miss Nicholas won the Dog Writers Association of America award for the Best Technical Book of the Year with her *Nicholas Guide To Dog Judging*. Then in 1979 the revision of this book again won the Dog Writers Association of America Best Technical Book Award, the first time ever that a revision has been so honored by this association.

During the early 1970's, Miss Nicholas co-authored, with Joan Brearley, five breed books for T.F.H. Publications, Inc. These were *This Is The Bichon Frise, The Wonderful World Of Beagles*

Anna Katherine Nicholas.

And Beagling, (winner of a Dog Writers Association of America Honorable Mention Award), *The Book Of The Pekingese, The Book Of The Boxer,* and *This Is The Skye Terrier.*

During recent years, Miss Nicholas has been writing books consistently for T.F.H. Included are *Successful Dog Show Exhibiting, The Book Of The Rottweiler, The Book Of The Poodle, The Book Of The Labrador Retriever, The Book Of The English Springer Spaniel, The Book Of The Golden Retriever, The Book Of The Ger-*

man Shepherd Dog, and *The Book Of The Shetland Sheepdog*. Most recently in this series she has completed *The World Of The Doberman Pinscher*, and *The Book Of The Miniature Schnauzer*, while *The World Of The Rottweiler* is nearing completion, all of these true "breed spectaculars." In the series of the book you are now reading she has done *The Maltese, The Keeshond, The Chow Chow, The Poodle, The Boxer, The German Pointer*, and *The Weimaraner*, and in co-authorship with Marcia Foy, *The Beagle, The Basset Hound*, and, now nearing completion, *The Dachshund*. In the T.F.H. KW series she has done *Rottweilers, Weimaraners* and *Norwegian Elkhounds*. She has also supplied the American chapters for two English publications, imported by T.F.H., *The Staffordshire Bull Terrier* and *The Jack Russell Terrier*, and an up-date chapter for the Labrador classic, *The Labrador Retriever* originally authored by the late Dorothy Howe.

In addition to her Dog Writers Association of America awards, Miss Nicholas has on two occasions been honored with the *Kennel Review* "Winkie" as Dog Writer of the Year, and in both 1977 and 1982 she was recipient of the Gaines "Fido" award as Journalist of the Year in Dogs for which, as a two-time winner, she now no longer is eligible owing to the regulations limiting the number of times one person can win the award.

Miss Nicholas's judging career, started in 1934 at the First Company Governors' Foot Guard in Hartford, Connecticut, has been and still is a distinguished one, taking her to a full schedule of engagements in the United States and Canada. She has officiated at all of the most prestigious events in both countries, and her numerous Westminster assignments have included that of being the third woman in history ever to judge Best in Show there, which she did in 1970.

These two Collie illustrations are from the 18th century. The upper one depicting a Rough Collie, the lower one a Smooth Collie.

This woodcut from 1653 is generally believed to depict a Collie of that period.

Chapter 1

Origin and Early History of the Collie

Collies come in two varieties, the Rough Coated and the Smooth Coated; both are bred to the same standard except for the coat. The rough variety had been the shepherds' dogs who protected and guarded the stock in pasture while the smooth variety were drovers' dogs who guided the stock on the trips to market.

Both types needed strength, good hearing and keen eyesight. The rough Collies, working in the cold climate of the highlands, and constantly on duty there, needed the warmth and protection of their heavy weather-resistant coats.

The value of these outstanding sheepdogs to people dependent upon pastoral pursuits in mountainous areas was inestimable. They were a necessity, and although pedigree records were not kept back in those days, it would seem fairly safe to think that as long ago as the 16th century, if not actually even earlier, thought was given to producing dogs best able to successfully pursue their work of guarding and herding farm animals. The keenness of the Collie's eye, for example; and of his hearing, the latter unquestionably aided by the shape of ear leather with the tip drooping slightly as the dog is at listening attention, forming a "sound box" to help pick up distant sounds: these important characteristics helped tremendously in making the early Collies so desirable and admired in the work of shepherds' dogs.

Ch. Ashtead Violetta, a gorgeous tri-color of fifty years ago in England, one of the famous "Ashteads" owned by Mr. R. H. Roberts.

The Collie takes his name from the sheep of Scotland, which were known as "colleys;" thus they became "Colley dogs." We have read that the rough Collie was of a smaller size than the smooth Collie, about 14 inches high at the withers; the early smooth Collie considerably more upstanding. Additionally the roughs were said to have possessed shorter, broader heads and that the majority were either solid black or black and white in color. During the 16th, 17th and 18th centuries, "Colley Dogs" were to be found in Northern England, and Wales, as well as in the Scottish Highlands.

The Collie remained a shepherds' dog until 1860, when the breed caught the attention of that great lover of dogs, Queen Victoria, who saw and admired the breed during a visit to Scotland, with the result that she acquired a lovely one. Thus it was that the Collie came to the Royal Kennels to join the other breeds represented there. Of course the Queen's acceptance of them quickly made Collies a stylish breed to own, with the eventual result that numerous breeders of them sprang to life throughout the country. Emphasis turned to the appearance of the dogs even beyond their usefulness. The Collie's increasing popularity continued, being but briefly interrupted during World War I, and on its way again upon the end of that period.

Tri-colors (black, tan and white), were the most usual Collie colors of the "early days" with blue-merles becoming quite numerous. Then came the day of the sable and white, of which a dog named Old Cockie was the first recorded, in the period around 1872. That started a run of popularity which led to the near extinction of the tris and merles, but then by the close of the 19th century the rarity of *those* colors led to concern and to several dedicated breeders working to restore the merles.

It was during the 20th century that some serious dog fanciers became intrigued with breeding Collies, and thus the organized keeping of pedigrees began. Much progress was made within a short period of time, the dogs becoming both more refined in type and larger in stature. Old Cockie has received much credit for stamping type on the rough Collie.

Ch. Kilmeny Jess, well-known Collie bitch from the late 19th century depicts the type so desirable at that period.

Soon after introduction of the sable color, many different Collie colors started to appear, among them buff, red, various mottled shades, and, of course, the sables; black, black and white (no tan), and tan and white.

By 1886, Collie type was quite well set in England, and that type has remained unchanged there right up to the present time so far as the standard for the breed is concerned.

Birmingham, England, might also be called a focal point for development of correct Collies during the latter 1890's. The first appearance of a Collie at an English dog show was in that city in 1861, and two years later the one class provided there for the breed brought six of them into competition. There was still just one class provided for the breed in 1871, but this time 17 competed. A dog called Old Mec was the first prize winner; Old Cockie was second. Just to prove my often-mentioned theory that dog show judging has not changed too greatly over the years, nor people's reactions, let me quote from Hutchinson's on this show. The comment there is that "Old Cockie was undoubtedly the better dog of the two although placed second in the awards at this (his first) show." Later he was Best Collie at Birmingham over a period of several years. Both of these dogs became famous, and would be found, should one research that far back, behind many present winners.

Old Cockie was offered for sale in 1875 at the Midland Horse Repository. Affixed to his collar were 21 plates recording the engraved names of the shows at which he had won. According to Hutchinson's he was purchased by Mr. G. Dean Tomlinson of Birmingham by whom he was retired from the show ring according to this source of historical information. Elsewhere we have read that Old Cockie had been originally shown by Mr. W. White of Sherwood Rise, and that the history of his origin has never been revealed. We have read also that this great dog's ownership changed twice when he was about six years of age. His eventual final purchaser, and the owner with whom he completed his lifetime, was James Bissell, another noted Collie fancier from Birmingham. By the time of his retirement, it has been said that his list of prizes had grown to more than 40.

The other most formidable show Collie of this era was the aforementioned Old Mec, a dog younger than Cockie, having been born in 1870 by which time Cockie was two years old. He, too, is

Ch. Ashtead Applause owned by Mr. Roberts of England. A handsome head-study from the early 20th century.

from a background unknown beyond the fact that his breeder was Peter Gerrard. A daughter of Old Mec named Meg was selected by Mr. Bissell for breeding to Old Cockie. This produced a bitch named Maude who was to make notable contributions to breed progress.

Other important Collies as the 19th century drew to a close included Old Cockie's grandson, English Champion Charlemagne, who was born in 1879. This dog became quite invincible in the show ring of the 1880's, dominating Collie winning for a period of about five years, the first half of that decade. The culmination of his show career came when, at 11 years of age, he was brought

Eden Extra belonged to Mr. Fred Robson and was an important British Collie of the early 1920's.

Ch. Wishaw Rival, a Collie from Wishaw Kennels owned by Robert Tait in Scotland back at the turn of the century. Note the beautiful type and quality of his dog, even "way back then."

Ch. Eden Blue Blossom, one of the famous Collies exported by Mr. F. Robson's British kennel to the United States in early 20th century.

The famous British Collie breeder, Mr. Stansfield, with two of the fine representatives, a Smooth and a Rough, of his world-renowned Laund Kennel.

15

from retirement back to compete in the Veterans Class at the Collie Club Specialty, going straight through to Best of Breed.

A gentleman named A.H. Megson became interested in Collies around 1882, determined evidently to assemble a large majority of the very best for his kennel. Obviously price was no object when Mr. Megson learned of a Collie he wished to own; thus he acquired some very famous members of the breed. Champion Ormskirk Emerald came to him for an incredible 1500 pounds from former owner T.H. Stretch; Champion Southport Perfection, bred by Hugo Ainscough, cost Mr. Megson 1000 pounds; Edgbaston Marvel cost him 500 pounds. The money spent on these dogs was well spent, however, if one had it to use in this manner, as obviously Mr. Megson did! Champion Ormskirk Emerald, although making a slow start in the show ring, defeated all the other "bests" of his era at the Birmingham Show in 1896. Champion Southport Perfection, born in 1892, was five times winner of the Collie Club's Challenge Trophy. His descendants included a son, Wellesbourne Councillor who in turn sired the excellent Champion Wellesbourne Conqueror, born in 1895, bred by William H. Charles, eventually exported to the United States.

It is interesting to note that highly successful Collie breeders M.P. Barnes and Hugo Ainscough were brothers-in-law. In later years, Mr. Ainscough with his wife became co-breeder of some of the world's most famous Pekingese, the Heskeths, which were outstanding winners in both England and America.

FURTHER DEVELOPMENT OF THE COLLIE IN GREAT BRITAIN

As the 20th century approached, specific strains of Collies were developing in Great Britain, clearly prepotent in type. Among the particularly notable producers was Champion Wishaw Clinker who became a great sire under the ownership of Mr. R. Tait. Another dog with whom to reckon was Mr. Hugo Ainscough's Champion Parbold Piccolo.

Clinker was the result of the breeding of the Ormskirk Agreement daughter, Last Rose, to Heacham Galopin who was to become a champion in the United States following his purchase by D.E. Gardner for his Illinois-based Ravenswood Kennels. Clinker became a famous British sire and winner prior to his exportation to the United States to join the famous Collies owned by J.P. Morgan for whom he had an exciting winning career. Clinker was grandsire of the notable English and American Champion Squire of Tytton, born in 1904.

Piccolo was born in 1899, bred by Mr. Ainscough, by Champion Wellesbourne Conqueror from Parbold Pinafore, descendant of Champion Matchley Wonder. Like Clinker, he was a highly successful show dog. Tragically, Piccolo, who had been exported to Mr. Behling for a very large price, disappeared soon after his arrival and was never seen again. He did leave behind him two sons, Champion Anfield Model and Champion Ormskirk Olympian who were also eventually exported to the United States.

In 1903 Mr. Tait brought out a marvelous dog in the tri-color Champion Wishaw Leader. Mr. T. Hurry the following year produced Champion Squire of Tytton who was a most beautiful sable and white.

Since the early 20th century, Mr. Fred Robson and his Eden Collies have been world famous. Back in December 1921, *Our Dogs* magazine in their Christmas Supplement ran a story on his Collies which is still interesting to read today.

At this time, Eden Extra was just fresh from successes at the Edinburgh dog show, from where he had returned home in triumph. He was on the way to his title with two Challenge Certificates to his credit, and he was already the sire of Champion Eden Elenora, Eden Eunice, Sybil of Sandy, and numerous other winners. We have read glowing accounts of Champion Eden Elenora's quality. She was then dam of a litter by Champion Poplar Perfection; her dam was Eden Emily.

Also from 1921, we have come upon a story of the Laund Collies, owned by Mr. W.W. Stansfield at Laund House, Rawtenstall, Lancashire. The success of this kennel, and its impact on future generations of Collies, would be difficult to overestimate as these dogs have been widely acclaimed wherever Collies are known. Both rough and smooth Collies from this kennel have been history-making. English Champion Laund Limit, a sable and white dog, was born in 1912 and one of the most famous of Mr. Stansfield's early Collies. He was the sire of English and American Champion Laund Logic, born in 1917, who was imported by Mrs. Florence Bell Ilch of Red Bank, New Jersey, for her Bellhaven Kennels during the early 1920's. In England, he left behind Laund Lucas who became the progenitor of the Lucason family at

Ch. Laund Logic,
one of the famous
Collies produced
at Laund Kennels
owned by Mr.
Stansfield.

The very famous Smooth Collie, English Ch. Laund Lynne, an outstanding winner who had many important honors to her credit, owned by Mr. Stansfield.

Ch. Laund Lindrum was owned by Mrs. R. E. James in England during the 1930's. An outstanding show and stud dog of his day.

Ch. Laund Lawson, Best of Breed Collie, Rough or Smooth, at England's Manchester Championship Dog show in 1932. Another striking example of the Laund Kennel's contribution in quality to the Collie breed.

The great winning early English Collie, Ch. Ashtead Applause, a handsome sable and white representative of Mr. Roberts's Ashtead Kennels, from where so many important dogs have come earlier in the 20th century.

Ch. Laund Lindrum illustrates No. 22 in a series of 25 champion dogs whose pictures were issued in the form of cigarette cards by Ardath Cork and State Express 333 Cigarettes.

Champion
Laund Lindrum
COLLIE
owned by
Mrs. R. E. James

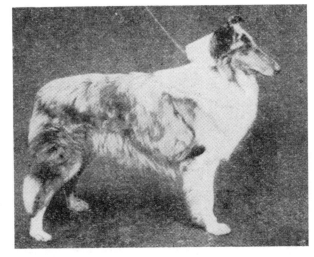

Ashtead Blue Ensign, owned by Mr. Roberts, was especially admired for excellence in head, forequarters and hindquarters. From Great Britain in the 1920's.

Bellhaven, so prominent during the 1930's. And Limit also was the sire of English Champion Alstead Luminous, born in 1914, who was imported to America by Mrs. Clara May Lunt, among whose other importations was the memorable English Champion Eden Emerald. Another notable dog owned by Mr. Stansfield was Champion Laund Logic with at least ten Challenge Certificates to his credit, also the winner of "Best Non-Sporting Dog" at the Kennel Club Show of 1920. Champion Laund Legislator won the Grand Challenge Class at Ayr in 1921, among many other important show successes. Laund Lightfoot, a puppy at that time, had earned the distinction of 33 first prizes in these classes. And the remarkable smooth merle, Champion Laund Lynne, had to her credit in the early 1920's 98 first prizes, eight Challenge Certificates, and on 28 occasions had gained the special for Best Specimen in Show, including the Lord Lonsdale gold cup for Best Bitch in Show at the Kennel Club's 1920 event, as well as the Pearson Silver Jardiniere for Best Non- Sporting Dog or Bitch.

This magnificent Collie is Ch. Wickmere Reveille, by Ch. Merrie Oaks Midnite Star ex Wickmere Wynken, handled by Mrs. George Roos. One of five champions for Midnite Star to have finished during 1965. Major and Mrs. George Roos, breeders-owners, Falls Church, Virginia.

Chapter 2

The Collie in America

The Collie reached America well before the 20th century, having been brought here by a number of the early settlers who needed them to tend their flocks as they had done in Scotland and elsewhere in the British Isles. The Collie Club of America was organized in 1886, only two short years following the organization of the American Kennel Club, making it one of the oldest kennel clubs in the United States, and the second parent club to become a member of the American Kennel Club (A.K.C.).

Classes were available for "Shepherd Dogs or Collie Dogs" at the second show held by the Westminster Kennel Club, and at Westminster's third event, two Collies who had been imported from Queen Victoria's Balmoral Kennels in Scotland were among the entries.

Development of the show Collie in the United States seems to have occurred almost simultaneously with the breed's development as show dogs in Great Britain. The breed did appear at dog shows in England some 17 years earlier than in the United States, but the fact that they were in competition in the American show ring at least a dozen years earlier than the turn of the century would seem to give the breed an almost American flavor since it preceded so very many others in recognition here. Perhaps it was this reasoning which led to Collies being included on the Centennial Postage Stamp, which, with this one exception, features breeds which actually originated here. For does not a century in America entitle the Collie to be thought of in the hearts of the American public as one of our very special breeds?

The beauty and intelligence of the Collie led to the breed's quick adoption by many prestigious Americans. J. Pierpont Morgan, the famed financier, imported some of the finest, including English Champion Wishaw Clinker and Ormskirk Galopin, both of whom had been born a couple of years prior to the turn of the century. Clinker was descended from English Champion Christopher, also imported by an American fancier, who had preceded him here when purchased by the Chestnut Hill Kennels belonging to Mitchell Harrison in Philadelphia, Pennsylvania. Ormskirk Galopin was a son of the famed English Champion Ormskirk Emerald ex Ormskirk Memoir.

The aforementioned Christopher has proven an enormously important dog in United States Collie history. His great-great grandsire was Trefoil, who was the sire of English Champion Charlemagne and was the patriarch behind some of the world's most important Collies.

It was in 1885 that the first Collie registered in this country was included in the American Kennel Club Stud Book. Many of these early Collies were American-bred, attesting to the fact that the breeding of Collies in the United States was being practiced then and prior to that time, with the English influence arriving here as the 1800's drew to a close.

A steady growth of interest was being recorded in the United States as the century ended. Registrations in the breed totalled 675 for 1900, and we understand that by this time about 30 Collies had earned their titles of champion here, about one third of them imported, the majority of dogs and bitches born in the United States. The first Collie Champion to have been born and bred in the United States was Roslyn Dandy, born in 1888.

The Collie Club of America (C.C.A.) was founded on August 26th 1886 with a charter membership numbering 58. The first President was Jenkins Van Schaick who held that office until his death three years later. The first Delegate to the American Kennel Club, and Vice- President for the Collie Club of America, was Thomas H. Terry. The Standard was drawn up, based on that of the English Collie Club: constitution and by-laws were established, and C.C.A. became the Parent Club for Collies in the United States.

In 1887 the Collie Club of America held its first Specialty Show and Sweepstakes with an all-breed show, that of the New Jersey

Kennel Club. Many special trophies were offered to be won three times, which they quickly were retired, and then replaced by others. Three are still awarded as perpetual trophies by the Collie Club of America at their Annual Specialty. The Morgan Cup for Best of Breed honors the memory of J.P. Morgan who served the club in many capacities until 1908 at which time he retired from showing dogs. The Hunter Trophy is for Best American-bred in memory of William C. Hunter, an early secretary of the Collie Club of America. The Shotwell Trophy is for the Best Brace in Show in memory of former secretary- treasurer J.D. Shotwell.

It was in about 1900 that Mrs. Clara May Lunt joined the Collie Club of America. Mrs. Lunt, serving as President from 1918-1921, was the first woman ever to hold this office. In 1908 it was voted that Smooth Collies should compete in dog shows on equal terms with Rough Collies.

Mrs. Lunt organized her Collie breeding activities under the kennel identification of Alstead, and her interest in the breed remained steadfast until she passed away in the 1950's. By 1920 she had become the leading American fancier of the breed and Alstead dogs appear with consistency in pedigrees dating back to that period. Probably the most influential of her dogs was English Champion Eden Emerald to whom the prefix "Alstead" was given upon her importation of this famous winner.

Dr. O.P. Bennett, Tazewell Kennels, Washington, Illinois, made an impressive contribution to Collies with his importation of Champion Parbold Picador, grandson of Champion Anfield Model. Picador was directly descended from the influential English dog Edgbaston Marvel, and sired Southport Seal (who became the dam of English Champion Magnet) as well as English Champion Laund Limit, who sired English and American Champion Laund Logic.

Samuel Untermeyer imported an exciting dog, English Champion Squire of Tytton, who gained an American title as well as proving influential on future generations.

Willard R. Van Dyck, of the Honeybrook Kennels, was a very famous early member of the Collie fancy. His Honeybrook Kennels produced many a winner, and Mr. Van Dyck himself was a widely respected authority on the breed.

Another eminent Collie authority, Edwin L. Pickhardt, started his Sterling Kennels during this same era in the mid-West; they

Ch. Merrie Oaks Black Acorn, by Ch. Merrie Oaks Humdinger ex Ch. Merrie Oaks Jubilee, winning the Working Group at Santa Clara Kennel Club in 1961. Bred, owned, and handled by Mrs. Edmund Mansure.

Opposite page: *(Top)* Bonnie Maid of Wooley's Lane, by Ch. St. Adrian Scarborough ex Saint Adrian Maid Madcap. She was owned by Mrs. W. Henry Gray. Winners Bitch at Morris and Essex in 1949. *(Bottom)* The great Ch. Laund Ebony of Killarty O'Bellhaven, one of the many "stars" imported by Florence B. Ilch for her famed kennel at Red Bank, New Jersey. Photographed in May 1949.

27

Ch. Merrie Oaks Shooting Star bred, owned, and handled by Mrs. Edmund F. Mansure, La Honda, California. She finished her championship by going Best in Show from the classes, the third from her litter to gain title, by Ch. Merrie Oaks Star Boarder ex Ch. Merrie Oaks Julep. Merrie Oaks was a leading and influential kennel of the 1950's.

did not draw to a close until several decades later when this gentleman, then a resident of Washington, Connecticut, passed away.

The lady whom I personally consider to have been "Mrs. Collie" since my earliest awareness of the breed was Mrs. Florence Bell Ilch, owner of the Bellhaven Kennels at Red Bank, New Jersey, who died early in the 1980's. What a success story, this one! And a word of credit must go, as well, to the interest and devotion of M.J. (Mike) Kennedy who, for so long as I can recall, was the kennel manager at Bellhaven. A marvelous Scotsman and a truly great Collie man in every way!

English Champion Laund Logic was imported by Mrs. Ilch during the early 1920's for Bellhaven, where he lost no time in becoming an American champion and assumed a place of importance at Bellhaven Kennels. He was a son of English Champion Laund Limit. A young son of Logic, Laund Lucas, also had a strong influence on Bellhaven being behind the famous Bellhaven Lucason line which emerged during the 1930's. Champion Starbet Strongheart too was purchased by Mrs. Ilch during the 1920's; he became an outstanding winner and a tremendously important sire. Strongheart was born in 1920, sired by English Champion Alstead Laund Luminous from Lansing Berta, and at Bellhaven he became the sire of Champion Bellhaven Stronghold and of the bitch who produced Champion El Troubadour of Arken for Lil and Charles Wernsman, Gaily Arrayed of Arken.

Bellhaven At Last, one of the handsome Bellhaven Collies photographed in 1949. His type speaks eloquently for itself. Bellhaven was owned by Mrs. Florence B. Ilch at Red Bank, New Jersey.

The great and famous Rough Collie, Ch. Stoneykirk Reflection, owned by Mr. and Mrs. John Honig, winning Best in Show at Middlesex County Kennel Club 1963. One of the most outstanding Collies of the sixties. Handled by William J. Trainor.

Ch. Glen Hill Whiffenpoof Song and his sire Ch. Glen Hill Dreamer's Nobleman *(right)* with owner Patricia Starkweather at Teaneck, New Jersey in 1959.

Ch. Gaylord's Flyer winning the Specialty Show of the Collie Club of Northern New Jersey, April 14, 1957. Frank H. Ashbey handled for owner, Dr. James H. Mangels, Jr.

Ch. Brandwyne's Needless To Say winning the Collie Club of Maryland Specialty in 1957. Owner-handled by Mrs. Trudy Mangels. Dr. Wm. J. Burgess, judge.

It was Mrs. Ilch who achieved what is generally considered to be the American dog show world's most prestigious honor, that of winning Best in Show at the Westminster Kennel Club event. She did so in 1929 with Champion Laund Loyalty of Bellhaven, who remains to this day the only Collie in history to have won the top award at this respected event.

A catalogue from Westminster eight years later, in 1937, brings us some interesting and impressive information. The Collie entry there numbered 66 dogs which were judged by Mr. Walter H. Reeves, *nearly thirty of them belonging to Mrs. Ilch!* Can you picture the beauty of this glorious galaxy of Collies resting regally on their benches at this event? Unforgettable, I assure you!

Mrs. Ilch's only entry as a special that year was Champion Bellhaven Black Lucason, homebred, born in 1931, by Champion Lucason of Ashtead O'Bellhaven. But in the *Classes* were the following: Champion Bellhaven Blue Majesty (by Champion Bellhaven Black Majesty ex Champion Laund Lilac of Bellhaven), Champion Bellhaven Standard Bearer (Black Lucason-Champion Bellhaven Lady Lector), Champion Bellhaven Son of Lector (Champion Bellhaven Lector-Lady Stronghold of Bellhaven), Champion Bellhaven Ben Hur (Lector-Bellhaven Bethlehem Beth), Champion Bellhaven Lector (Champion Laund Lector of Bellhaven-Bellhaven Lady Lucason), Champion Bellhaven Luckystone (Champion Laund Luckystone of Bellhaven-Champion Eden Edith of Bellhaven), Champion Bellhaven Loyalty II (Champion Laund Loyalty of Bellhaven-Champion Bellhaven Bo-Peep), Champion Eden Blue Blossom of Bellhaven (Eden Electron-Pelton Blue Frizetta), and both a brace and a team from Bellhaven Kennels.

As recently as the 1960's we have found Bellhaven Collies entered at Westminster. More than 100 champions were bred by Bellhaven.

Another Collie breeder of tremendous importance and long duration in the Fancy was Mrs. William H. Long, Jr., founder of the Noranda Kennels on Long Island. Her foundation included a bitch from Bellhaven, a Lodestone bitch, and one from Marie Leary's Cosalta Kennels, the latter usually remembered more for her German Shepherds than for this breed. Champion Noranda Daily Double was one of Mrs. Long's greatest. He was a multiple Best in Show winner (all-breeds) and a Specialty winner with numerous Group successes as well. Champion Ink Spot of Noranda was a dog I greatly admired, to whom I awarded first in the Working Group at a North Westchester Kennel Club Dog Show some years back. Champions Cadet and Invader of Noranda were others who brought great honor to their breeder.

Mrs. Long was the founder of Dogs for Defense during World War II. She owned the first champion Collie to earn a C.D.X. title as well, Champion Master Lukeo of Noranda, who was sire of Silhouette of Silver Ho. The latter was sold to Nancy Caldwell for whom she became the foundation of Silver Ho Kennels.

Mrs. Long loved all of the Collie colors, and at one period owned dogs of each of the four at the same time. She was a lady who liked to enjoy her dogs "for the pleasure of their company." Her kennel was always kept small, and Mrs. Long had numerous housepets in her Collie family. A very respected lady, Dorothy Long was an admired judge and closely involved with club work, especially in the Long Island Kennel Club and the Collie Club of America, both of which she served as President.

An additional Long Island fancier whom we recall with admiration was Mrs. W. Henry Gray whose Wooley's Lane strain reached very special prominence during the late 1940's. Among her renowned Collies were littermate bitches, Champion Wooley's Lane Leal and Champion Wooley Lane's Electra. Leal achieved the exciting honor of going from the classes to Best of Breed at the National Specialty, defeating in the process numerous dog specials. Only several Collie bitches have reached such heights at the National, making this victory all the sweeter.

Saint Adrian Collies were owned by Mr. and Mrs. James Christie at North Hanover, Massachusetts, and became a force in the breed with which to reckon. Champion Beulah's Golden Sultan was imported by these fanciers from Mrs. Nadine George of England. Sultan was a three-time Best of Breed winner at the National Specialty, having gained this honor in 1941, 1942 and 1944. Mrs. Christie was widely admired for her knowledge of the breed, and her interest in it continued right up until the time she passed away at the beginning of this decade.

What student of Collie history has not read about the Arkens, made famous by Mr. and Mrs. Charles A. Wernsman of Derby, Connecticut? Charlie and Lil Wernsman (friends whom I held in most affectionate esteem) and I became acquainted through their fabulous Afghan Hounds, who were every bit as outstanding as

At the Keystone Collie Club Specialty 1957. *Left,* Mrs. Trudy Mangels handling the bitch Ch. Gaylor's Petty Girl for Dr. James Mangels. *Right,* Capt. E. H. Conklin owner-handling Ch. Fancy Hi Honeybrook However.

their Collies. They perfected strains of truly magnificent dogs in both of their breeds, for which they deserve a round of sincerest applause.

The Arken Collies began back in the early 1920's with the purchase of a nine-month-old puppy bitch, Halbury Jean, sired by Champion Halbury Aviator (grandson of English Champion Magnet) from Halbury Expession. Jean herself not only became a champion, but she became the dam of six champions plus the excellent dog who was never shown due to a nose injury, El Capitan of Arken.

El Capitan, although himself without a show career, surely earned a place of honor in Collie history. His son, Champion El Troubadour of Arken, born in 1930 from Gaily Arrayed of Arken, became the sire of 15 champions. Gaily Arrayed was a daughter of Champion Bellhaven Big Heart.

Champion Future of Arken, born in 1931, was by Champion El Troubadour of Arken from Champion Nymph of Arken (from Champion Halbury Jean) who was the dam of four champions in addition to Future, these including Champion Cock Robin of Arken who was acquired by Tazewell Kennels where he became an important sire under Dr. Bennett's ownership. To Future goes credit for being the sire of five champions, two of them among Colliedom's most influential: Champion Honeybrook Big Parade,

Ch. Black Hawk of Kasan, famous smooth-coated Collie, taking Best in Show at York Kennel Club in 1970 for Sandra K. Tuttle, owner. William L. Kendrick, judge. Miss Leslie Canavan, handler.

Noranda Distinct Echo, by Ch. Brandwyne's Destiny's Echo ex Distinctly Nora-
nda, a handsome puppy from the mid-1960's owned by Mr. and Mrs. Wm. H.
Long, Jr., Noranda Kennels, Oyster Bay, New York. Winner of Best Bitch in
Sweepstakes, Collie Club of Long Island.

Int. Ch. Noranda Daily Double, famous winner of the mid-1960's, bred and
owned by Mr. and Mrs. William H. Long, Jr., Noranda Kennels, Oyster Bay,
New York.

Ch. Shirhaven Noontide Nimbus, by Arrowhill Ace High ex Ch. Shirhaven Lucious Lollipop, C.D., owned by Shirhaven Kennels, Wynnewood, Oklahoma. Nimbus was a multiple Best of Breed winner, including half a dozen or more Specialty Shows of which five were during 1961, and also had a dozen or more Group placements.

who made history for William Van Dyck; and Champion Sterling Stardust, who did likewise for Edwin L. Pickhardt.

Champion Honeybrook Big Parade was a breathtaking dog, the sire of 17 champions and a three-time winner (1935, 1936, and 1939) of Collie Club of America National Specialties. Honeybrook Helen was his dam, she by the Bellhaven-owned Aalveen Anchor ex Gene of Arken, El Troubadour's half sister.

Big Parade carried on the tradition of his family by becoming a respected sire, two of his best known progeny having been Champion Astolat Peerless who was influential in the Sterling line, and

Ch. Erin's Own Gold Rush winning Best of Breed at Keystone Collie Club Specialty 1962. Owned by Lorraine A. Perry, handled by Brian Carabine. Dr. Richard Greathouse judging.

Champion Silver Ho Shining Arrow, the only male in his litter from Nancy Caldwell's Silhouette of Silver Ho (Dorothy Long's breeding). On the strength of Silver Arrow's quality the breeding of Silhouette to Big Parade was repeated, this time producing Champion Arrowhill Admiral of Silver Ho.

The Champion Silver Ho Shining Arrow line has continued on down through the decades. From Stephen J. Field's bitch, Lodestone Bandoliera II, came Champion Silver Ho Parader, of whom we are well aware for his record of producing producers as well as winners. The Parader line stands on its record in the Collie world and continues to the present day through such descendants as his son, Champion Parader's Golden Image; Champion Parader's Bold Venture (by Image); Champion Parader's Country Squire (by Venture); Champion Two Jay's Hanover Enterprise (by Squire):

Int. Ch. Noranda Daily Double bred and owned by Mr. and Mrs. William H. Long, Jr., Oyster Bay, New York. Handled by Miss Leslie A. Canavan to Best in Show, Framingham District Kennel Club, June 5, 1966.

and on into the current winners that you will read about in the following kennel stories.

It is also a Champion Silver Ho Parader son who became the sire of Champion GinGeor Bellbrooke's Choice, with 30 or more champions to his credit, of whom you will also read frequent mention in the kennel stories.

We have endeavored to bring you a comprehensive background of the people and dogs who stand behind the most excellent Collies of today. Ideally we would like to tell you of each and every one of them, but lack of space prohibits this. We are sure that you will find much to interest you in the kennel stories which bring the background up-to- date, and join with us in a salute to all who have contributed toward the creation of our almost breathtakingly beautiful Collie of the present.

Ch. Dorelaine' Smooth Domino, by the famed Ch. Black Hawk of Kasan ex Dorelaine Star Miss, bred and owned by Doris Werdermann. Photo taken in 1969.

Chapter 3

The Smooth Collie

As previously mentioned, the smooth variety of Collie developed alongside the roughs, coat being the only physical difference between the two varieties. We understand that at the turn of the century quality was about equally good between the two varieties in England, but that the smooths had not attained the popularity of the roughs.

It was Mr. Megson, so well-known for his magnificent Roughs, who was among the first to enter a smooth specifically bred for the show ring, and he did so with one who became English Champion Pickmere, a rough-smooth cross tri-color, whose breeder was F. Hurst.

English Champion Heathfield Dot is another familiar name to the researchers of early smooth history, whose sire was a rough brother of English Champion Metchley Wonder, her dam a smooth working bitch named Blue Light.

In 1900 along came English Champion Babette of Moreton, almost entirely smooth-bred, and a great granddaughter of Champion Heathfield Dot. This bitch created considerable admiration and furor when, in 1902, she won Best Collie of Any Variety, beating out the Rough, at the Collie Club Specialty Show.

The early smooth of whom we have read the most glowing accounts is Champion Laund Lynne, a blue merle daughter of Herman from Primly Primula. Born in 1917, she was owned by W.W.

Stansfield. This bitch won the splendid total of 16 Challenge Certificates and also accounted for Best in Show All Breeds or Best Bitch in Show on 95 occasions! Among her trophies was the one for Best in Show All-Breeds at an English Kennel Club event. In addition, she also earned the silver trophy offered by the Kennel Club to be awarded for the three- time winner of Best Bitch in Show. Her show career was never interrupted for maternal duties, but at the age of ten years she was bred and raised seven puppies.

It was in 1888 that smooth Collies first appeared at a dog show in the United States. This was at the Westminser Kennel Club where the lone entry competed *not* against rough Collies but in a class for smooth-coated Collies and bob-tailed Sheepdogs! As the century turned, both varieties of Collie did compete together at Westminster, with only the open class divided by coat.

The earliest American champion smooths of whom we have found records were Champion Clayton Countess who finished in 1906; Champion Ormskirk Mabel in 1907, followed by her daughter, Champion Ormskirk Lucy in 1908, and Champion Warran Patience in 1909.

Throughout the decades of the 1920's and the 1930's, interest in smooth Collies came to a standstill, the roughs attracting the attention of any and all who were interested in the breed. As the 1930's drew to a close, the pity of this became apparent to some of the true lovers of the entire Collie breed, who formed a syndicate in order to revitalize interest in the smooths. Those doing so were H.R. Lounsbury, Mrs. Lunt, Robert G. Wills (the Bob Wills so popular in our present-day judging rings), Arthur Foff and Mrs. Genevieve Torry Eames. Two excellent smooths were imported from the Laund Kennels in England, a tri bitch named Laund Loftygirl and a blue dog, Laund Blue Peter, syndicate members breeding the two and drawing lots for the puppies. After two litters which generated only disappointing interest, the group disbanded. However they had made a very real contribution to smooth quality in the United States through these Smooths and their descendants as a study of pedigrees of the variety in the present day makes abundantly clear.

The American Smooth Collie Association was founded in 1957 due largely to the efforts of Miss Margaret Haserot, owner of Pebble Ledge Farm in Ohio, a fancier of the smooths since the 1920's. The club started with only about two dozen members, but today

Ch. Glocamora Morning Mist, a top winning Smooth Collie of the 1960's, had at least 25 Bests of Variety. Owned and handled by Isabel Chamberlin, Doylestown, Pennsylvania.

Beautiful head study of the Smooth Collie Sumerhill Special Delivery. Best of Breed at three Specialties over numerous rough coated champions, this son of Ch. Sumerhill Inherit The Wind and Shadaglen Call the Wind is also a multiple Group placement winner. El Solo Kennels, Richard and Marjorie Norstrom, Honolulu, Hawaii.

has become a thriving organization with more than 200 active fanciers on the membership roster. The smooth is making its way up the ladder of breed popularity, and many outstanding ones are to be seen in our show rings.

Miss Haserot's own smooths go back to the Laund Kennels in England through her homebred Little Dorrit, who was from her English importations Laund Lavender ex Laund Larchfield. Bred to the blue smooth Halmaric Baronet, a son of the pair imported from Laund Kennels by the syndicate, Dorrit produced a tri-color smooth, Halmaric Trilby, who produced the first smooth in nearly four decades to gain championship in the United States, Cham-

This handsome Smooth Collie is the dog, Ch. Black Hawk of Kasan, who was bred by Sam E. Singer, Jr. and Ethel C. Singer. Owned by Sandra K. Tuttle, Black Hawk was sired by Ch. Highman of Arrowhill ex Ch. Kasan's Fine and Fancy. An all-breed Best in Show winner. 1968 Best of Variety, Collie Club of America.

pion Pebble Ledge Bambi. Born in 1944, Bambi was by the rough Champion Halmaric Scarletson. She became a noted winner during the 1940's, I believe winning Best of Variety each time shown, and she produced the two smooth champions: Christopher of Pebble Ledge and Pebble Ledge Inca, C.D., littermates by the rough Champion Harline's Son of Cainbrooke.

My good friend Alice Burhans, whom I came to know and admire while writing my *Book of the Shetland Sheepdog*, shares her interest in Shelties with an equally constructive one in Collies, particularly the smooths. Alice was the breeder of the littermates Champion Belle Mount Bambi C.D. and Lulubelle of Belle Mount

This is El Solo Karob The Bare Facts as a puppy, age six and a half weeks. Owned by the Norstroms and Mr. and Mrs. Robert Frost.

who both played a strong role in development of the Smooth Collie we know today. These bitches were by Luke of Pebble Ledge (son of Champion Pebble Ledge Bambi) from the rough Noranda-Tokalon bred bitch, Belle Mount Rosey Future.

Belle Mount Bambi was owned by Tom Kilcullen and completed her bench championship with four Group placements, setting a record for her variety at the time. She was undefeated among the Smooths, and was Best of Opposite Sex to Best of Breed at a Chicago Specialty.

As a producer, Bambi became the dam of the noted sire Champion Cul-Mor's Kilcullen of Ebonwood, whose progeny includes nine champions, and his littermate Champion Cul-Mor's Babette of Ebonwood. Another among the several additional champions from Bambi is Champion Echo of Ebonwood, C.D.

Bambi also won the Dog World Award for Canine Distinction for obedience where she gained the title C.D.X.

Lulubelle, too, did her share for future generations of smooth quality.

It is interesting to note that in 1982 Alice Burhans and her daughter Rebecca had the pleasure of owning the first Smooth Collie to place in a Working Group at Westminster, Champion Christopher of Ledge Rock, who placed third, handled by Rebecca.

It was early in the 1960's that the smooths started really coming into their own. Since then some very outstanding dogs and bitches have been produced and exciting wins accomplished.

Others who contributed to Smooth Collie progress in the early days include Mr. and Mrs. Omer Rees, whose Glengyle Kennels, based on importations from England, are in California, and who did much to bring correct type and quality to the breed there. Myrtle Ackerman, a founding member of the American Smooth Collie Association, Inc., was a successful and devoted breeder who produced numerous champions from her Myrack dogs, on Long Island, New York. Isabel Chamberlin when active in the breed produced and owned many famous Collies of both varieties. Her blue smooth bitch, Champion Glocamora Morning Mist, bred by Vikki Highfield, won numerous Bests of Variety, Group placements, and twice was Best of Opposite Sex at Collie Club of America Specialties.

Irene Kneib is another who was noted for fine smooths, several dozen champions, at least 13 of them smooth, having brought fame to her kennel since the early 1930's.

You will find some very famous smooth champions among our illustrations, and also included in our kennel stories in the pages of this book.

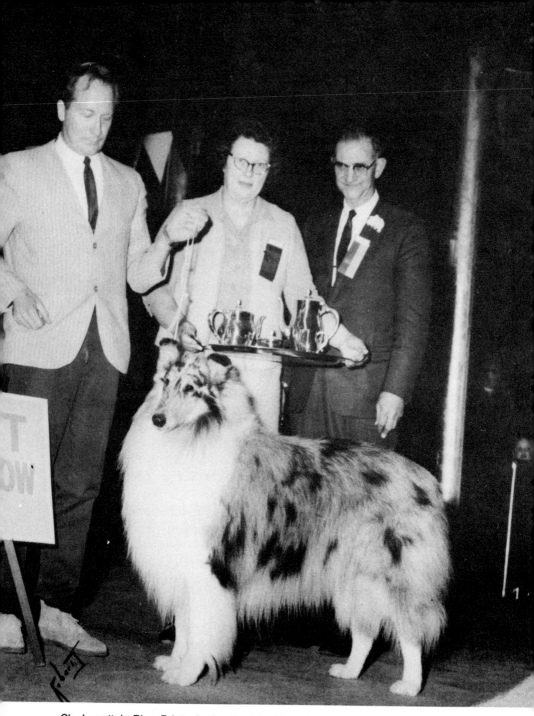

Ch. Lunette's Blue Print winning Best in Show for Billy Aschenbrener, Abbehurst Kennels, Sherwood, Oregon.

Chapter 4

Collie Kennels in the United States

ABBEHURST

Abbehurst Collies are at Sherwood, Oregon, where their owner, Billy Aschenbrener, has owned and/or raised a number of very beautiful and impressive members of this lovely breed.

Two of the early "stars" were born back in 1947, and helped to provide excellent background for the Collies who would follow there.

Champion Pleasant Hill Enchantress was a daughter of Champion Blackout of ToKalon ex Pleasant Hill Blue Horizon, and was bred by A. Lee Perry. The first time shown, while still a nine-month-old puppy, Enchantress created considerable excitement by going Best in Show all-breeds—a notable achievement! She completed her championship with Best of Breed at a Specialty Show held in conjunction with an all-breed event, then finished the day with first in the Working Group. As a producer, Enchantress also did the job well. She had champion progeny to her credit, plus a Best in Show winning grandson.

Champion Pleasant Hill Torch Song was a homebred who more than did Billy Aschenbrener proud! She was a daughter of Black Sheik of Cainbrooke from Pleasant Hill Highlite. She completed her championship in four consecutive shows, finishing by taking Best of Winners and Best of Opposite Sex at the 1949 Collie Club of America Specialty, where 250 Collies were in competition. She

Ch. Pleasant Hill Torch Song *(left)* and Ch. Pleasant Hill Enchantress with their owner Billy Aschenbrener.

was an all-breed Best in Show winner in both the United States and Canada.

As a producer, Torch Song was the dam of several champions, had a Best in Show grandson, and is to be found 'way back in the pedigrees of many top winning Collies of the current generation.

Champion Abbehurst Again was born in 1960, a homebred by Champion Random's Future Forecast ex Franluart Francine. Shown on only five occasions to gain her championship, she went on to become 'an outstanding Best of Breed and Specialty Show winner.

Champion Lunette's Blue Print was an exciting dog, bred by Harold Goodman, whelped in 1962. He was a champion at less than one year old, and became a Specialty and all-breed Best in Show winner. As the sire of several champions, Lunette's Blue Print still has descendants among the top winning Collies today.

These are just a few of Billy Aschenbrener's Collies, but they give you an idea of the type and quality to be found in his kennel.

Ch. Lunette's Blue Print, by Ch. Three Trees Beau Blue ex Ch. Lunette's Chloe, born in 1962. Pictured winning Best in Show, Reno Kennel Club 1967. Bred by Harold Goodrich and owned by Billy Aschenbrener.

Ch. Pleasant Hill Enchantress *(left)* and Ch. Pleasant Hill Torch Song; two famous winners owned by Billy Aschenbrener, Abbehurst Kennels, Sherwood, Oregon. From a painting by Lorraine Still.

Fun time! These puppies at play are by Ch. Windarla's World Seeker ex Sunnybrook's Etched in Ebony (from the Parader line). Marlene Nicholson, owner, Hendersonville, Tennessee. Photo by Lynn Sanders.

ALLIANCE

Alliance Collies, at Hendersonville, Tennessee, are owned by Marlene and Ewing Nicholson. This kennel has the honor of being the home of the all-time Top Winning Collie in the history of the breed, a record spanning 98 years of Collies shown in the United States.

This dog is Champion Windarla's World Seeker, born April 28, 1978, bred by Arlene and Luwinda Webb, handled by George E. Schlinker. Sired by Champion Windarla's Worldly Wise ex Windarla Presents The Blues, World Seeker has won more Bests of Breed, more Group Firsts, and more All-Breed Bests in Show than any other Collie on record. He was No. 1 Collie (All Systems) in 1981, 1982, and 1983, during which period he also retired the Sterling Silver Bannerblu Trophy as the Top Blue Merle Collie three years in a row; No. 6 Herding Dog (Routledge System); No. 7 Herding Dog (Kennel Review System); and Best in The South for the *Collie Review* Award 1981, 1982, and 1983. The show ring total which brought World Seeker to the top is truly amazing. His Best of Breed total stands at 267; his Group placements number 166, including Best Working Dog on 23 occasions and Best Herding Dog on 36 occasions; he was seven times a Best in Specialty Show winner, and ten times has taken all-breed Bests in Show.

The Nicholsons also are the owners of World Seeker's sire, Champion Windarla's Worldly Wise, by Champion Wickmere Chimney Sweep from Champion Windarla's Sweet-N-Lovely.

Ch. Windarla's World Seeker surveying his domain in March 1984. The picture of regal elegance as he watches activity on the lake. Marlene R. Nicholson owner. Photo by Lynn Sanders.

Bred by Arlene and Luwinda Webb, Worldly Wise was handled by Sherri and Bob Schmidt. He was a Working Group winner, and No. 12 Collie (Hawkins System) for 1975 while being campaigned.

Other notable Collies owned by the Nicholsons include Belle's Alliance With Venus, who should by now be finished as she lacked just one point of title as we were writing—a daughter of Champion Tamarack Eclipse (Champion Tamarack Asterisk son) from Lakshmi's Magic, C.D. (Champion Hanover's I Am Legend daughter).

Then there is Canadian Champion Kairlake Moonlight Sonata, by Canadian Champion Shamont Silver Dollar (Champion Ravette's The Silver Meteor son) ex Canadian Champion Lickcreek's Classic Rythm.

Alliance's Wonder Whirl, C.D., by Chris Mik's Jim Beam ex Edenrock Diamond In The Ruff, co-owned by Marlene Nicholson with Donna M. Barrett, has the distinction of being a Best of Breed winner from the puppy classes. Wonder Whirl is one of at least several Alliance Collies who have distinguished themselves in obedience competition, others including Silcrest Xtriordenaire, by Champion Wickmere Silver Bullet ex Silcrest Silver Myst.

A current young "star" is Champion Alliance's Amiable Amy, by Henderson's Dandy Man, who is World Seeker's full brother, from La Creek's Gold Alliance (daughter of Champion Tamarack Eclipse and granddaughter of Champion Hanover's I Am Legend. Amy has been bred to World Seeker after gaining her title in a spectacular manner including Best of Winners at the 1984 Chicago International, which should produce some exciting future winners for the Nicholsons.

AZALEA HILL

Azalea Hill Kennels are owned by Mrs. Richmond Fairbanks, a highly successful Collie breeder who resides at Greenville, South Carolina.

Hanover's Love Song, 1969-1982, was a bitch of tremendous importance to the development of Azalea Hill. When bred to the great sire, Champion Two Jay's Hanover Enterprise, a litter brother to her granddam, Love Song produced four champions, all of them subsequently producing champion progeny of their own that are carrying on in what has become the family tradition.

Hanover's Love Song, an important producing bitch for Azalea Hill's Collies of Mrs. Richmond Fairbanks, Greenville, South Carolina. The dam of six champions, all of whom subsequently produced champion offspring of their own.

Ch. Azalea Hill's Mr. Christopher taking Group 1st under noted Collie breeder and authority Mr. Roy Ayers in 1977, owner-handled by Mrs. Richmond Fairbanks, Greenville, South Carolina. Bred by Eugene and Carol Chapman. This famous producing sire is the double grandsire of two Group winning tri bitch specials currently in competition.

Love Song's title-winning sons and daughters include Champion Azalea Hill's Mr. Christopher, who is an all-breed Best in Show winner. Ranked No. 2 Collie for 1978 under the Kennel Review System and No. 3 under the Hawkins (Collie breed) System, it is interesting to note that in this same year, the Collies ranking No. 1, No. 2, and No. 3 were all sired by the great Champion Two Jay's Hanover Enterprise. Among Mr. Christopher's honors, in addition to the all-breed Bests in Show, have been Best of Breed at seven Specialty Shows and multiple firsts in the Working Group, back in the keenly contested groups before Working and Herding separated.

Eugene and Carol Chapman bred Mr. Christopher, who has made an imposing record as an outstanding sire. He is the double grandsire of Champion Azalea Hill's Canebrake Cameo and Champion Canebrake's Lucky Lady, both of whom have two Specialties apiece and Group firsts as we go to press.

Champion Azalea Hill's Marianne, who was also from Love Song's litter by Hanover Enterprise, goes down in Collie history as the dam of Champion Azalea Hill's Top Man, winner of a Collie Club of America National Specialty in the smashing entry of 450 Collies, 76 of which were specials.

Ch. Azalea Hill's Mr. Marcus, bred by Mrs. Richmond Fairbanks and owned by Marianne Zeshonski, winning the Working Group under Wm. L. Kendrick at Columbia Kennel Club in 1978.

Marianne's daughter, Azalea Hill's Honey Love, was Top Producing Collie Bitch for 1980, made so by her three American and one Canadian champions in her first litter. The brother was Top Winning Male and the sister Top Producing Bitch the same year.

Bred back to her grandsire (Champion Two Jay's Hanover Enterprise), Honey Love produced Champion Azalea Hill's Flair, Champion Azalea Hill's Mr. Marcus, Champion Azalea Hill's Windhover, Canadian Champion Azalea Hill's Aviator, and, with 12 points, which include a major, Azalea Hill's Princess Feather.

Of the above, Champion Azalea Hill's Mr. Marcus became a Group winner who completed his title in a very creditable manner, gaining his first major in the form of a Working Group first and his second by going Best of Breed over specials from the classes at the Collie Club of Louisiana Specialty. As "frosting on the cake" he was always owner- handled.

Champion Azalea Hill's Strike Force, by Champion Azalea Hill's Court Jester ex Summertime's Hanover Special, started his show career as a puppy with a 5-point major under noted breeder-judge Mr. Lee Collins, won his class at the Collie Club of America National Specialty, and finished his points at the Collie Club of Greater Memphis Specialty.

Champion Shadow Hill's Stormy Sea, C.D.X., not only has starred in conformation competition but in obedience as well. He has to his credit both Specialty and Group awards under George Schlinker's handling, one of his most exciting weekends having been the occasions on which he won back-to-back Working Groups at the big Atlanta and Macon shows.

Champion Azalea Hill's Top Man was Best of Breed at the 1980 Collie Club of America National Specialty, also becoming the Nation's No. 1 Collie for that year. Bred by Mrs. Fairbanks, he is co-owned by her with Mr. and Mrs. T.C. Livingston of San Antonio, Texas handled by George Schlinker. Both his sire, Champion Tartanside the Gladiator, and his dam, Champion Azalea Hill's Marianne, were National Specialty Show winners.

Champion Azalea Hill's Future, by Champion Azalea Hill's Mr. Christopher ex Melodyland Genir of Skywalk, gained one of his majors by going Winners Dog at a Collie Club of Georgia Specialty, going on to become the winner of Group placements.

Currently winning for Azalea Hill as we write is the widely admired Champion Azalea Hill's Canebrake Cameo, a tri-color bitch

This lovely puppy became Ch. Azalea Hill's Future. Here at seven months old, he is owner-handled by Mrs. Richmond Fairbanks to give us a beautiful example of a very handsome young Collie.

who has multiple Group Firsts and Specialty wins to her credit. She is handled by Wade Burns for her owner.

Champion Azalea Hill's Landstar is another handled by Mr. Burns whose wins in specials and in Group competition are adding up in a very satisfactory manner. Mrs. Fairbanks co-owns Landstar with the T.C. Livingstons.

Champion Azalea Hill's Sheyne, a Court Jester son from Honey Love, is also enjoying a rewarding career, this one handled by Jon Woodring.

Azalea Hill, as can readily be seen, is an active, busy kennel bringing forth many lovely Collies.

Ch. Barksdale Bullseye, by Ch. Wickmere Silver Bullet ex Ch. Highefields Debutante, a blue male from a litter of four champions. Nancy McDonald, owner, Manassas, Virginia.

BARKSDALE

Barksdale Collies are owned by Nancy McDonald at Manassas, Virginia, who has the distinction of being co-breeder with Mary Fields of a very notable litter of four champions sired by Champion Wickmere Silver Bullet from Champion Highfields Debutante.

Included in the litter are Champion Barksdale Best Dressed, who won back-to-back Specialty majors, was First in Open Tri Dogs at the Collie Club of America in 1981, and now belongs to Arnold and Bobbie Redding at Expert, Pennsylvania.

The other three littermates are all owned by Nancy McDonald, for whom they have brought some exciting honors to Barksdale. For example, Champion Barksdale Early Light, who was No. 1 Rough Collie bitch in 1981, finished as a puppy, transferred into specials, then really started rolling. She was Best of Breed at the Collie Club of Long Island, Best of Opposite Sex at San Gabriel Collie Club, Collie Club of Maine, and the California Collie Club among other Specialty and Group placement awards.

Champion Highfields Whispering Hope finished with three majors as a puppy, then became the dam of the Best Puppy in Show at the Collie Club of America National Specialty in 1982.

Champion Barksdale Bullseye won four points and two major reserves as a puppy and is now being seriously campaigned.

As for Best Dressed, his honors have included winning the Collie Club of Maryland Specialty and that of the Mason and Dixon Collie Club on consecutive days under judges Yoshio More of Japan and Mrs. Roz Durham, respectively.

CONRAD

Conrad Collies were founded in the 1950's by Mr. and Mrs. Roy L. Ayers of Stone Mountain, Georgia, who have long been devoted fanciers of this breed.

The foundation cornerstones here were provided by the stunning dog, Champion Poplar Stop The Music, purchased from Mary Beresford, Poplar Kennels, Rhinebeck, New York, and the excellent bitch, Champion Conrad's Sweet Expression.

Stop The Music was not a champion when purchased; Roy had the fun of personally making him one, which must have been his first.

Sweet Expression was a homebred, and when she gained her title she thus became the first homebred Collie bitch in the state of Georgia. She was bred only to Champion Stop The Music, and she produced champions in every litter. She was never shown by anyone except Roy Ayers and his daughter Linda.

These two Collies and their progeny dominated the winners circle for many years between the 1950's and 1969, and contributed well to Collie progress in the South.

Champion Poplar Stop The Music was a double grandson of Champion ToKalon Storm Cloud, being by Poplar By Storm ex Champion ToKalon That's For Me. A mahogany sable himself, he

BEST
LOCAL
DOG

Fourth victory for Roy Ayers's Collies retired the important A.D. Alexander Perpetual Trophy in 1957! Truly an exciting occasion as any Collie enthusiast knows. This picture brings you Roy Ayers (whose smile has not changed a bit over the years!) with the judge, Mrs. Harold Thorpe, then President of the Collie Club of America. The trophy was retired by Conrad's Sweet Expression, Conrad's Music Maestro, and, for two wins, Conrad's Dancing In The Dark. All of these Collies went on to become champions. Dancing In The Dark is pictured.

sired both sable and tri-color and he produced many champions and point winners both from linebreeding and from complete outcrosses.

Champion Conrad's Music Maestro was by the foundation dog and bitch, Storm and Sweet Expression. He completed his championship taking Best of Breed for a 5-point major at the Collie Club of Georgia Specialty after less than a year of showing with 20 points. A series of Bests of Breed and Group placements followed.

Two of the Conrad Collies won the "Best in the South" award for the Ayers on two consecutive occasions. And Stop The Music and Music Maestro have both been used to illustrate the ideal Collie in *Dog World* magazine.

Conrad's Mister Sandman was the last Collie bred and shown by Roy L. Ayers. He was exhibited only once, at ten months of age, and was Winners Dog, Best of Variety, and third in the Working Group on that occasion. After this show, the Ayers retired all of their dogs as Roy's judging assignments were keeping him increasingly busy and he preferred, under those circumstances, not to remain an exhibitor.

Ch. Conrad's Music Maestro, all-breed Best in Show winner, who, in 1956, won more Best of Variety and Group placements than any other Collie in the United States. Winner of "Best in South" Award for 1956. Owned by Conrad Kennels, Mr. and Mrs. Roy L. Ayers, Stone Mountain, Georgia.

Conrad's Theme Song was bred by Roy L. Ayers and sold to a kennel in Puerto Rico for whom she won Best in Show there.

DEEP RIVER

Deep River Collies are at Pittsboro, North Carolina, where they belong to Kathy V. Moll.

The first champion owned by Kathy was Champion Azalea Hill's Windhover C.D., whom she co-owned with Mrs. Richmond Fairbanks of Azalea Hill Kennels. By Champion Two Jay's Hanover Enterprise ex Azalea Hill's Honey Love, this handsome dog has been a successful winner shown in specials as well as a notable sire.

The first homebred champion of Kathy Moll's was, strangely, from a litter of one and the first litter she had bred. This was Champion Deep River's Even Chance, C.D., a sable male who finished with a 4-point major at an all-breed show and a Specialty

Ch. Stoneybrook Silver Saint, C.D., No. 6 Collie in the United States for 1983, was bred by Betsy C. Winberry and owned by Kathy V. Moll and Mrs. Richmond Fairbanks.

major at the Collie Club of Louisiana Specialty. He was by Champion Tartanside the Inheritor ex Azalea Hill's Dark Angel, C.D.

Among the famous winners at Deep River we find Champion Stoneybrook Silver Saint, C.D., who finished at age two years with two Specialty majors and a Reserve Dog at the National Specialty to his credit. In 1983 this dog was the No. 1 Collie in the United States, Hawkins System, and he is a multiple Specialty Best of Breed winner and a Group winner. Saint was bred by Betty C. Winberry and is owned by Kathy V. Moll and Mrs. Richmond Fairbanks.

In addition to his own success in the show ring, Silver Saint has proved to be a highly successful sire. Among his promising youngsters is Champion Deep River Satin Slippers, who gained a 4-point major her first time in the ring at just six months' age. Deep River's Silver Standard, from Lizdon's Merry Frolicker, is a pointed son of Saint who as a young puppy won an all-breed Best in Match Show, and in three weekends of showing at championship events gained three major reserves.

Champion Canebrake Lucky Lady is a tri bitch who completed title in 12 shows with just two and a half months of showing. In the current year, she has six Best of Variety wins, a Group fourth, a Group First and two Specialty Bests of Opposite Sex.

Deep River Collies are beautifully presented in the ring by Wade Burns and Jon Woodring.

EL SOLO

El Solo Collies are owned by Richard and Marjorie Norstrom and are located in Honolulu, Hawaii.

Marjorie purchased her first of the breed about ten years ago, in the mid-1970's, from the Northwest area of the mainland. This was Colleen, a daughter of American and Canadian Champion Lachlan Thunder O'Shane from Angelic's Thoran of Random, who came down from the Bellhaven line. Colleen was never a conformation dog, but she did very well in obedience where she gained her C.D. She was bred, at five years of age, to Champion Heritage Ringmaster, producing one puppy whom the Norstroms call Zeni.

Before and during her interest in Collies and Shetland Sheepdogs, Marjorie Norstrom was a very active cat fancier who bred and showed Siamese. Unfortunately, in time she developed an al-

Shane's Colleen O'Shamrock, the first Collie at El Solo Kennels in Hawaii, owned by Richard and Marjorie Norstrom at Honolulu.

lergy to the cats which necessitated discontinuing her association with them. As she could not quite bring herself to give up cats completely, she purchased a copper-eyed white Persian. During the cat's stay in quarantine, her owner met and became friendly with a group of Sheltie owners, from which event her interest in Shelties and Collies started and grew. Presently she is working with Shelties through the High Born, Robert Bruce, and Peter Pumpkin lines.

It was in 1979 when Marjorie Norstrom attended a Collie Club of America Specialty Show which was held in San Diego. There she saw what she considered to be THE dog—Champion Glenecho Set The Style, by Champion Tartanside The Gladiator ex Glenecho Style O'Shadaglen, bred and owned by Dick Moffatt. At the Specialty he finished in grand style, taking Winners Dog and Best of Winners. Today almost every Collie at El Solo is related to him.

Ch. Glenecho Royal Dynasty, by Ch. Sumerhill Inherit the Wind ex Glenecho Summer Melody, owned by El Solo Kennels, Richard and Marjorie Norstrom, Honolulu, Hawaii.

Top Dog in the El Solo Kennels is undoubtedly American and Canadian Champion Akirene's Counter Force, who is by Set The Style from Canadian Champion Berridale Akirene Misty Morn. A multiple Best in Show, multiple Group and multiple Specialty Best in Show (six of them consecutively at the time of this writing) winner, he has been in the Top Ten among all breeds in the state of Hawaii for more than three years, and is No. 1 Collie in the state. He completed his title in four Hawaiian shows, all majors.

The first champion sired by "Kane," as Counter Force is known, is a lovely rough tri bitch, Champion El Solo Kane's Triple Treat, and several others who were well on the way should now be finished. As we write, Kane himself is with his handler, George Schlinker, being shown on the mainland's East Coast.

Champion Summerhill Inherit The Wind is a notable Smooth Collie who heads this variety at El Solo. This is a sable male who joined the family in 1983 and has been campaigned by Brian Phillips on the West Coast. A son of Champion Glenecho Set The Style from Champion Sumerhill the Winds of Chance, he is a multiple Group dog with both firsts and placements to his credit. His career as a sire is just getting under way, and we understand that Mrs. Lois Hillman has an exciting litter of nine by him.

Champion Braetana Let It Shine is a blue merle smooth bitch by Set The Style from Braetana Verra Blue. Bred by Jane Akers, she came to the Norstroms all the way from Montana to quickly finish title in her new home.

Champion Glenecho Royal Dynasty is the sire of the first Smooth Collie puppies to have been born in Hawaii. He is by Champion Summerhill Inherit The Wind ex Glenecho Summer Melody (who is a litter sister to Set The Style), and he completed his championship in Hawaii with three 5-point majors. He now has three Group 3rds, a Specialty Best of Variety, and a Specialty Best of Breed.

Champion Summerhill's Special Delivery, sable Smooth male, is another very distinguished member of this kennel. An Inherit the Wind son from Shadaglen Call the Wind, he attracted considerable attention by going Best of Breed at three different Specialty Shows under three specialist judges (Mrs. A. Wharton, Mrs. L. Walker, and Mrs. R. Durham), defeating numerous Rough champions in the process. He is also the winner of multiple Group placements.

Summerhill's Heir Express is the dam of the first Hawaiian-born Smooths, and her second litter will have arrived prior to the appearance of this book. She is by Inherit the Wind from Call the Wind.

A young bitch being watched with interest, co-owned by the Norstroms with Mr. and Mrs. Robert Frost, is El Solo Karob The

Ch. El Solo Kani's Triple Treat, by Am. and Can. Ch. Akirene's Counter Force ex Champion Solo Leni The Happy Hour, is the first champion bred by Marjorie Norstrom.

Bare Facts, by Glenech Royal Dynasty ex Summerhill's Heir Express. She has already a spectacular Best Puppy to her credit at a recent Collie Club of Hawaii Specialty.

Although the Norstroms may have seemed to be more or less concentrating on Smooths, this is not the case for along with them the Roughs rate high in interest, too. Champion El Solo Zeni the Happy Hour is a Rough tri-color bitch who did her share of winning, and is now producing champions. She is by Champion Heritage Ringmaster ex Shanes Colleen O'Shamrock, C.D. (the original bitch at El Solo). Several Rough bitches are co-owned with other fanciers, one of Parader breeding, and two Counter Force daughters, one from Zeni, the other from Champion Windrift's Dream Weaver, C.D.

A recent addition is Mainstay Leather 'N Lace, by Cantigair's Counter Punch from Paradices Brolly By Golly. An elegant sable and white bitch, she promptly won a 4-point major at a recent Specialty. She was purchased from Keith Dooley.

The Norstroms are doing their best to breed sound, well balanced and stylish Collies—both Rough and Smooth. Obviously they are succeeding admirably.

Zeni herding the geese. Owned by Marjorie S. Norstrom.

ELEGY

Elegy Collies are owned by Mr. and Mrs. Kenneth S. Goldfarb at Ballston Spa, New York.

Ken Goldfarb had been a Collie fancier since the early 1950's, had finished approximately ten champions, was a licensed judge (now retired), an American Kennel Club delegate, and Chairman of the A.K.C. Trial Board for several years (now retired also from A.K.C. commitments) when he and Mrs. Goldfarb were married. His kennel prefix in those days was "Cagy."

As Mrs. Goldfarb had never been a "dog person," and as they were living then in a New York City apartment, immediately following their marriage in 1960 the Goldfarbs had only one Collie, a smooth named "Roger" who was officially Champion Macdega Point Blank, and was their pet. With Ken's judging assignments, the Goldfarbs had occasion to attend many dog shows, and associated with many of Ken's Collie friends, particularly the couple who were to become Lynn Goldfarb's mentors, Ben and Isabelle Butler of Kinmont Collie fame.

Lynn became increasingly fascinated with the concept of breeding and showing (and hopefully was storing all the education at her disposal in the deep recesses of her mind, much of which she hopes is still to surface). The eventual result was the Goldfarbs' purchase of two puppy bitch littermates: a blue called Bonnie and a tri called Eve, known as "Big Blue" and "Pink Pad" as a play on the then SOS-Brillo soap pad rivalry advertising. Bonnie and Eve, who were American and Canadian Champion Elegy in Blue and Ebony Elegy respectively, lived with the Goldfarbs in the Murray Hill section of New York City where they were fortunate enough to have a second floor apartment with a 40' by 50' terrace overlooking the area once occupied by the Collies raised by J.P. Morgan during the early 1900's. These puppies were a delight to their owners, whose once fashionable terrace became host to a dog house and the decorative shrubbery quickly became stumps.

When the puppies were a year old, it was decided to breed them: Bonnie to Champion Tartanside the Gladiator and Eve to Kinmont Ritchie. This brought the Goldfarbs' New York City life to an end, and they then moved their possessions and hopes to Ballston Spa, a little town near Saratoga Springs where they formerly had maintained a vacation house.

The first litter brought the Goldfarbs some memorable times— like the day their eight-month-old puppy, Dondi, went to the big 1975 International Kennel Club Show in Montreal. Their 4 a.m. departure from home brought them to the morning Collie Specialty, where Dondi started towards becoming Canadian Champion Elegy Distant Drummer by taking Best of Winners for five points. That afternoon the Collie competition at the all-breed show saw Dondi add to these laurels by taking Best of Breed (and of course Best Puppy) over a nice turnout of specials for a second five-pointer. He then won the Puppy Working Group, later heading for home with the necessary ten points for Canadian Championship, thus just requiring a win under a third judge to complete title, which he did a month later, again going Best of Breed over the specials and winning the Working Group. What a lovely accomplishment for a puppy 8-9 months old! One of the saddest events of Lynn Goldfarb's life with Collies was the loss, following an operation for torsion, of this beloved dog at only three years of age! She truly felt as though she had lost her greatest friend, as from the very beginning Dondi had been her special dog.

Dondi left a legacy in his then three-month-old son, Scott, who was to become Champion Elegy Drumbeat, C.D. As a puppy, Scott won all the Working Groups at the matches, then went along to become a champion at 16 months of age. Besides being "king" at Elegy, Scott looked after all puppies from the time they were a few weeks old, playing with them, sharing their food dishes, teaching them manners and cleanliness. He intervened in all squabbles, and protectively straddled the underdog defensively. No dog has ever challenged him.

Since Scott was so special and Lynn wanted to give him some show attention, and because she wanted to see what the obedience routine was like (especially to find out why so few Collies competed in obedience and why, when present, so many had a hang-dog look about them) Lynn decided to start working Scott in obedience, with the much needed help of a friend in training. He proved to be a quick and willing worker, exceedingly smart, and to Lynn's satisfaction, so happy about the whole experience. He obtained his C.D. title in six shows, despite the ineptness of his handler (to quote Lynn's words). She was gratified to find that a Collie could do a fine obedience routine in a gay and happy manner.

Scott produced some wonderful puppies, including his son, Champion Elegy Disco Drummer (Dusty) who is noted for a most typical and gorgeous head and expression. A relatively young dog, Dusty in his turn is passing along much of his own good quality. Scott also produced Elegy Crescendo (Mike), who produced five Smooth Collie champions in one litter when bred to Champion Jancade Misty Blue. She herself was No. 2 Top Winning Smooth Collie in the U.S. for 1978.

Queen at Elegy is American and Canadian Champion Elegy in Blue (Bonnie), one of the already-mentioned foundation bitches who is now 11 years old (early 1985) and as spirited as ever. Bonnie is full of *joie de vivre*, and just loved the shows. She has her own story about finishing. Her Canadian Championship had been attained as a puppy, and she had one major and numerous other U.S. points when she went on the Florida circuit with the Goldfarbs' handlers in pursuit of her American title. At the first show, a Collie Specialty, she went Best of Opposite Sex, gaining her few remaining necessary points over the next several days. Having finished, she was pulled from the remainder of the shows, which broke the major at those still to follow (at that time it was not yet permissible to move a finished dog up to specials). Those on the circuit pleaded with the handlers to show her in order to save the major, which they refused to do. They did, however, permit a ten-year-old little girl to take a completely ungroomed Bonnie into the ring. But Bonnie was not about to be shunted aside! She took the little girl, who was completely inexperienced in showing dogs, around the ring, barked when she wanted more liver, and set herself up for the judge. After winning the Open Blue Class, someone at ringside noting the situation took pity and groomed Bonnie before the Winners class. Now Bonnie was truly preened for success, taking the little girl back into the ring and stealing the show. She went Winners Bitch, the little girl was thrilled, and Bonnie happily proud of her accomplishment. Needless to say, the request to show her was not repeated.

In raising and showing dogs, Lynn Goldfarb comments, all does not invariably turn out as it should. One of the most beautiful of bitches owned by the Goldfarbs was Kinmont Elegy, just about perfection in head, sound, and well put together. She, though, was not destined to finish, probably due to her not having had the high spirit that makes so great a difference with a show dog. Her *forte* was in the whelping box, where she became the dam of Elegy Crescendo who produced five smooth champions. She is also the dam of Champion Elegy Aida who, after being moderately campaigned, was rated No. 12 in the scale of Top Winning Collies in the United States for 1981.

The Goldfarbs' basic concept in breeding and raising Collies revolves around the theory of developing wholesome minds and bodies. They believe the best possible breeding is made by taking into consideration the physical virtues of each dog. The pedigree is only something the Goldfarbs feel should be considered in the recesses of one's mind. The breeding must be based on the individual dogs, their characteristics and their needs, not the great-grandfather's characteristics. Too, the Goldfarbs do not limit themselves in line- breeding. Accomplishing the successful breeding is only the first step. Then the puppies must be nourished physically and emotionally. Elegy puppies are talked to, gently wrestled and hugged from the time they are two weeks old. Great pains are taken to develop a Collie who can cope with all situations without fear and can freely give love. The feeling of the Goldfarbs is that this is important for the pet you sell as well as for the show dog you are raising.

GLEN HILL

Glen Hill Collies had their inception in Haverford, Pennsylvania, one of the lovely and historic Main Line suburbs of Philadelphia. When Patricia Starkweather began the serious breeding of Collies, she lived in an ancient stone manor house. On the gray granite gate posts were carved the words GLEN HILL 1881. The name of her home became the family name of her Collies, to whom she has devoted most of her life. Her own name at that time was Patricia Shryock, which was already famous in the Collie world prior to her becoming, by marriage, Patricia Starkweather.

The first Glen Hill Collie to make a name for herself was Champion Glen Hill Dainty Miss, who fulfilled her owner's dearest wish by taking Best of Winners and Best of Opposite Sex at Westminster in 1953! The Westminster Show had become Patricia's idea of Mecca since childhood when she read the fascinating Collie stories of Albert Payson Terhune.

Many champions followed Dainty Miss, and they have left an important mark on the breed. The male of the Glen Hill line who

Ch. Glen Hill
Emperor Jones (Ch.
Glen Hill Dreamer's
Nobleman son), has
been a strong
influence on the
breed through his
son Ch. Glen Hill
Full Dress and his
grandson Ch.
Anrum's All The Way
II. Owned by Patricia
Starkweather,
Middleburg, Florida.

became the greatest source sire, and who is still in the tail male line of every Glen Hill Collie, was Champion Glen Hill Dreamers Nobleman. This glorious sable and white dog finished at Westminster in 1959, then went on to take Best of Breed there, owner-handled, the following year. Nobleman then went second in the Working Group at Westminster, a placement that has not been equalled since then at Westminster to the present day. Nobleman won most every Specialty Show and innumerable all-breed shows to become the Top Winning Working Dog in the United States at that time.

While Nobleman sired many champions, his most influential son was Champion Glen Hill Emperor Jones. This gorgeous tricolor sired the most dominant sire of the late 1960's, Champion Glen Hill Full Dress.

The influence for good which Full Dress introduced is now spread throughout the breed. Most of the top winners at the Collie Club of American Specialty for the past few years have been direct descendants of Full Dress. Among these are Champion Tartanside The Gladiator, who was three times Best of Breed at the National Specialty; Champion Tamisett Golden Dream; Champion Shamone Storm Along; Champion Carnwath Evergreen; Champion Carnwath The Great Pretender; and Carnwath Thrilled—all of them National Specialty winners who trace closely to Full Dress.

Other outstanding Collies from this line include Champion Glen Hill Show Boy, winner of the Blue Banner award for the Top

Ch. Glen Hill Dreamer's Nobleman winning Best of Breed over 128 Collies at the Collie Club of Long Island Specialty. Owned by Patricia Starkweather and William B. Lex, Jr.

Winning Blue Merle in the country, 1979, awarded through the Collie Club of America. Show Boy was a top breed, Specialty and Group winner. One of the *great* winning males directly from Full Dress, through his son, Champion Glen Hill Star Ridge Star Dust, was Champion Glen Hill Prototype. He came from a half brother-sister breeding of Champion Glen Hill Star Dust to Champion Glen Hill Blue Dress. From this came four champions: Prototype, Champion Glen Hill Lavendar Blue, Champion Glen Hill Silver Lace, and Champion Glen Hill Star Ridge Blue Lace. Many leading Collie kennels in the United States, Canada and South America have built their winning stock on dogs from this combination.

Ch. Glen Hill Cramer's Empress in 1964. Finished as a puppy, then produced Ch. Glen Hill Emperor's Double Up and Ch. Cramar's Empress Coulotte in her first litter. Patricia Starkweather, owner.

This great producing bitch, Ch. Glen Hill Blue Dress, when bred to her half brother by Ch. Glen Hill Full Dress, (Ch. Glen Hill Star Ridge Star Dust) became a leading dam by producing four champions. Later bred to Ch. Tartanside The Gladiator (who goes back twice to Full Dress) produced Ch. Heritage Shade n Silver. Patricia Starkweather, owner.

The line still continues to flourish today at Glen Hill, located now in Middleburg, Florida, near Jacksonville. The premier stud at present is Champion Glen Hill Flash Back, so named for his great resemblance to Champion Glen Hill Full Dress to whom he traces back nine times. A daugher, Champion Glen Hill Campus Cutie, finished her championship in April 1984 with a notable win at the Collie Club of Georgia Specialty. She is the 29th Glen Hill champion. However, more than 100 champions trace directly to the line.

Patricia Shryock Starkweather is the author of the widely acclaimed book, *All About Collies*, now in its third revised edition. She writes the Collie column for *Dog World* magazine, which she had done for the past 26 years. Additionally she has written for *The American Kennel Gazette*, for *Collie Cues*, and for the Collie Club of America *Bulletin*, the latter in 1981 gave over an entire issue to the Glen Hill line of Collies.

HAMPTON

Nowadays Virginia Hampton is one of our busiest and most respected multiple breed judges, which is how she is best known to fanciers who are new to our dog show world. Virginia, however, has also been a long-time Collie breeder and exhibitor and there have been some very notable Collies at her home in Doylestown, Pennsylvania.

We bring you photos of several of the homebred-owner-handled Collies with which Mrs. Hampton did some nice winning during the 1960's. Her dogs were very widely admired and certainly a credit to her as an accomplished breeder who enjoyed handling her own dogs in the ring.

Ch. Hampton Hallmark Honor Guard, by Hampton Hallmark ex Hampton Hotcha Cha, bred, owned, and handled by Virginia Hampton. The sire of four champions and four additional point winners.

Ch. Hampton Honor Guard's Heiress pictured taking her second 4-point Specialty win, Best of Winners, and Best of Opposite Sex at the South Jersey Collie Club Specialty, June 1964, under judge George Dahl. Bred, owned, and handled by Virginia Hampton.

IMPROMPTU'

Impromptu' Collies are owned by Barbara Schwartz whose husband, Dr. Martin Schwartz is supportive of her efforts. Located at Hollis, New Hampshire, for more than fifteen years, Impromptu' Farms prior to that time, dogs and family have moved and lived throughout the country.

Although Barbara has owned Collies since she was eight years old, the beginning of this venture really started in Detroit in 1961. Barbara made an *impromptu* purchase of a pet Collie puppy named Clifford Brown as a wedding gift for Martin. Clifford remained a beloved canine member of the family for 16 years. A move to the Boston area in 1963 for Martin to attend postgraduate school introduced this couple into the world of dog shows. Clifford did win some classes, but the Schwartzes knew that he was not a "show type" Collie. The purchase of a bitch who also turned out not to have show quality convinced them that more study and experience were necessary before another purchase should be made.

Another move, this time to New York City, gave Barbara an opportunity to study many Collies and the chance to visit some of the legendary kennels in the area. Several of the old, big kennels were still active then, and Barbara and Martin were able to visit these establishments and learn from their owners. It was an invaluable experience.

Finally in 1965 another Collie puppy was purchased. This tri daughter of Glen Knolls Knightswood Sky ex Bayberry Brandy Alexandra was Crown Royal Midnight Mood (Maggie to her friends), and it was she who became the foundation of Impromptu' Collies. Several years later, her litter sister, Noel's Gold Skyward Destiny, was purchased and when bred to Champion Impromptu' Mingus Destiny (a Maggie son) produced Champion Impromptu' Instant Carmine and his sister, Impromptu' Sunshine Showers. They are important aspects in today's Impromptu' Collies.

Crown Royal Midnight Mood was bred to Champion Glen Knolls Flash Lightning in 1966, producing Champion Impromptu' Repartee, Champion Impromptu' Burnt Norton, Champion Impromptu' Hocus Pocus, and Archalong Miss Perfidy. Repartee was Best of Winners and First Futurity Finalist at the Collie Club of America Specialty in 1967 and Best of Opposite Sex there in 1969. Burny Norton was Best in Show at the Western Pennsyl-

Ch. Impromptu Burnt Norton, by Ch. Glen Knolls Flash Lightning ex Crown Royal Midnight Mood, was Best in Show at the Western Pennsylvania Kennel Club 1971. Bred and owned by Barbara Schwartz. Shown by Tom Coen.

vania Kennel Club Dog Show in 1971. Hocus Pocus became the dam of two champions. Miss Perfidy was the dam of one champion.

A repeat of the Flash Lightning-Midnight Mood breeding took place later, producing Champion Impromptu' Mingus Dynasty, who sired two champions before his death at only two years of age, and Champion Impromptu' First Edition.

The next move for the Schwartzes, owing to army obligations, took Impromptu' Collies to Lawton, Oklahoma. Two years of breeding and showing in the Southwest gave Barbara and Martin an intensive education into canine movement and health problems. Visits to many large and small mid-Western kennels gave them an even greater appreciation of the Collie.

Ch. Impromptú Richochet as a puppy. This Collie, Brandwyne's New Legacy ex Ch. Impromptú Repartee finished title in 1970. Bred by Barbara Schwartz.

Ch. Impromptu Repartee, by Ch. Glen Knolls Flash Lightning ex Crown Royal Midnight Mood. First Futurity Finalist, Winners Bitch and Best of Winners, Collie Club of America 1967. Best of Opposite Sex, Collie Club of America National Specialty 1969. Dam of four champions. Bred and owned by Barbara Schwartz, Hollis, New Hampshire.

In 1967 Champion Impromptu' Repartee was bred to Brandy-wyne New Legacy. In this litter of five were Champion Impromptu' Rendezvous, Champion Impromptu' Raconteur, and Champion Impromptu' Richochet. The latter became the sire of 16 champions and highly influential in the breeding programs of numerous kennels today.

For her next litter, Repartee was bred to Champion Brandy-wyne Barberry Mister. In it was Champion Impromptu' Kudos (one of the basic crosses used by Impromptu' to maintain type).

In her last litter, by Marklyn's Ring Round The Moon (son of Mingus Dynasty), there were two bitches important in present day Collies. Repartee had only eight living offspring; four of them became champions.

A move East, first to Dunstable, Massachusetts, and finally to Impromptu' Farm in Hollis, New Hampshire, gave the Schwartz family (by then enlarged by two children) a permanent base. In 1970 Barbara Schwartz was named Collie Breeder of the Year, the result of five Impromptu' champions having finished their championships. The same year she was approved by the American Kennel Club to judge Collies. In 1980 the Collie Club of America awarded her a Certificate of Special Recognition for outstanding service for her work on Coronavirus and Parvovirus.

Children have cut into the family dog showing for Barbara and Martin, but not their interest in or the breeding of their Collies.

In 1973 Champion Impromptu' Instant Carmine finished his title and in 1974 Champion Impromptu' Kudos finished his. The cross between these two sires, one the son of Mingus Dynasty, the other the son of Repartee, form the basis of the Impromptu' type. Crosses to the Richochet grandsons, Champion Laurien After-hours and Champion Laurien Afterhours Blues produced Champion Impromptu' The Silver Bullett in 1971.

Barbara Schwartz decided in 1976 that an outcross was needed. Several were tried, the most successful being the breeding of Impromptu' The Sorceress, by Instant Carmine from Impromptu' Magic (by Kudos ex a sister to Instant Carmine) bred to Champion Vi Lee's Platinum Plutonium. Although there is not one common ancestor in more than eight generations, Barbara felt that Vi Lee dogs resembled her own phenotypically. Through the years she has been impressed by the similarity of the head types and beauty of the dogs. The resulting litter of eight puppies produced Impromptu' The Haunting who has nine points, who was in turn bred to Impromptu' Apogee of the Moon (Kudo from an Instant Carmine daughter). Three daughters from this combination have been kept. One of them, Impromptu' Devil's Delight, was bred to the Richochet grandson, Champion Clarion's Light Up The Sky and they produced Champion Impromptu' Banner Still Waves, who was Winners Dog at the 1984 Collie Club of America Specialty at one year of age. Crosses to his aunts, as well as other Impromptu' bitches, constitute the breeding basis for the future.

The aim of Impromptu' Collies has been to breed an identifiable line of Collies that excels in beauty, type, elegance, head and expression, soundness, and a *joie de vivre*. It is, Barbara Schwartz comments, an ongoing quest.

JAYBAR

Jaybar Collies at Pickerington, Ohio, are a new kennel off to a very nice start for owners James and Joan Barrett.

The first champion and the foundation dog here is Champion Barrett's Mr. J.R., whelped February 21, 1979, by Champion Egbert's Perfect Reveller and J.J.'s Brittany. J.R. completed title, owner-handled, at the age of two years. Among his credits are Best of Breed at the Collie Club of Southern Ohio Specialty, plus Best of Variety on some 25 other occasions, and Best of Opposite Sex four times.

Currently the Barretts are starting out a new young bitch, Barrett's Forever 'N Blue Jeans, bred by Joyce C. Huff and born January 1983. This is a daughter of Champion Woodlands War Paint from Woodlands Sheer Vanity, and she swept through her early match shows with considerable flair. Now she is working for her title, which it is hoped she will soon attain.

LISARA

Lisara Kennels, owned by Carmen and Lawrence Leonard, are located at Rockwell, Texas. This couple has bred more than 37 Collie champions in addition to owning some half dozen more, and their successes have been numerous with both smooth and rough members of the breed.

A stand-out dog here is the very famous homebred smooth, Champion Lisara's Morning After, who finished her championship at nine months of age with four majors, four times Best of Variety over specials, and one Best in Sweepstakes. As of May 15, 1984, she had won an all-breed Best in Show, six Specialty Bests in Show, eight times Best of Variety and Best of Opposite Sex to Best in Specialty Show, First in four Groups, a Group Second and a Group Fourth.

Morning After won the Collie Club of America National Specialty Best of Variety in 1982 at 13 months old, and again in 1984, where she was also Best of Opposite Sex to Best in Show and Best Smooth Brood Bitch. As frosting on the cake, her son, at nine months' age, was Best of Opposite Sex to her on this latter occasion. He is now Champion Avrygeth Lisara Liaison.

Going back ten years in Lisara history, we find another renowned and exciting Smooth Collie, Champion Lisara's Scheherazade, who was born in 1973 and became the No. 1 of the Variety for 1975 under the Hawkins System. This one had two Specialty Bests in Show to her credit. Scheherazade was also homebred, by Champion Lisara's Merrytime Drambuie ex Tawny Miss of Glenayre.

Champion Lisara's Seaview Nightingdale is a third Smooth of very special note from this kennel. She was born in 1975 by Champion The Blue Baron of Arrowhill ex Champion Seaview's Lark of Kasan and in four litters produced 13 champions. Very nice going indeed!

Among the Rough Collies to be found at Lisara is Group winner Champion White Cloud's Bewitch'n Harvest, who was born in 1978 and is a stunning representative of the breed.

MARINER

Mariner Collies are owned by Margaret and James C. Vohr of Northfield, Massachusetts, and have been prominently in the limelight since the mid-1970's.

American and Canadian Champion Shamont Stormalong takes "pride of place" among the Collies at this establishment, an honor to which he does full justice. This handsome son of Champion Berridale Macdega Mediator ex Champion Shamont Sabrina was born in 1976, bred by Linda C. Sanders.

On the way to his American title, Stormalong took Winners Dog at the Collie Club of America Specialty in 1978. Since then he has become a leading Specialty and Group winner, having

The magnificent rough Ch. Shamont Stormalong, born 1976, by Ch. Berridale Macdega Mediator ex Ch. Shamont Sabrina, bred by Linda C. Sanders and owned by the Mariner Kennels of Peg and Jim Vohr. Winner of 29 Specialty Best in Show awards and the sire of 12 or more Rough Collie champions.

topped the breed 131 times in the United States, including 29 times at Collie Specialties! Always owner-handled, he has been on the Top Ten Collie lists for several years, and was awarded *Collie Review* magazine's Best in the East rating over four consecutive years, 1979 through 1982. A record for the magazine. His latest achievement was completion of his Canadian championship.

Currently Stormalong is the sire of more than a dozen Rough Collie champions. These include two recent additions to the list, the sable male Champion Piney Branch Octobersong, bred and owned by Pat Loos, Piney Branch Collies in Virginia, and Canadian Champion Carnwath Here I Am, a blue merle bitch bred and owned by Sue Symington, Toronto, Canada.

Octobersong is from Shamont Peaches 'N Cream, and he is a Group winner with several Specialties already among his credits.

Here I Am is from the Canadian Best in Show bitch, American Canadian Champion Carnwath Platinum Filagree.

The background of any successful kennel is in high quality bitches, and here Mariner again shines with Champion Shamont Sand Castles, C.D., born in 1974, and her daughter, Champion Mariner Castles In The Air, born in 1979.

Sand Castles is a half sister to Stormalong, being a daughter of his dam, Champion Shamont Sabrina. She was Winners Bitch at the Collie Club of America in 1976, and has won several Specialty Bests in Show. Sand Castles earned her C.D. when nine years of age, doing so at three consecutive shows. She is the dam of three Rough Collie champions, two of whom are Group winners.

Castles In The Air, Sand Castle's daughter, was sired by Stormalong and has proven a credit to both of her prestigious parents. She completed her championship with two Specialty majors and won seven Group Firsts during 1983; since that time she has added another Group and a Specialty Best in Show.

The Vohrs also own Champion Mariner Barnstormer, a litter mate to Castles In The Air, who is another Group winner at Mariner.

TRAVLER/JO CAN

Travler Collies at Clay, New York, were started in 1968 by Steve Tehon and his daughters Becky and Candy. The Tehons had owned Collies since the early 1950's, and they needed a puppy to begin to take over for their twelve-year-old tri. After a visit to River Odes Kennels, they found it impossible to resist a pretty sable bitch of Gin Geor lines who just happened to be of show quality. Of course they showed her, and from then on were "hooked"!

From this bitch's only litter sired by Champion Gin Geor Jack of Tamarack, came Champion Travler's Flim Flam Man. He was Candy's dog for Junior Showmanship; winner of the open sable class at the biggest Collie Club of America National Specialty ever; and Veterans Class winner as well as the oldest dog in the show at the Springfield Collie Club of America National Specialty; plus doing a stint in commercial work as cover dog and centerfold for a kennel run advertising brochure.

The Tehons' next major addition was a four-month-old sable bitch from Steve Field's Parader Kennels. "Mandy" grew up to become Champion Parader's Contented Travler, C.D.

Currently "best girl" at Travler is Champion Twin Creeks Mouse That Roared TT, a daughter of the all-time top sire, Champion Twin Creeks True Grit and a full sister to the excellent producer Champion Twin Creeks Post Script. "Mouse" is co-owned by Travler with Jo Can Collies, the latter the "spin-off" formed when Candy Tehon married Joe Ardizzone.

On the smooth side, the Tehons' first venture into this Collie variety was Candy's purchase of the future Champion Curtacy Wayward Wind from Hannah Cook's Curtacy Collies. A litter co-bred with Hannah resulted in three smooth champions, one at Travler/Jo Can and two at Curtacy, plus one other with several

Standing at attention inside the ring. Ch. Travler's Flim Flam Man owned by the Tehons, Clay, New York.

Ch. Parader's Contented Travler, C.D., foundation dog at Travler's Kennels, Rebecca L. Tehon, Clay, New York.

points, from a litter of five. Jo Can's current smooth winner is Champion Lisara's One and Only, co-owned with Carmen Leonard.

Currently both kennels are limited in what they can keep; just seven adults at Travler and seven or eight at Jo Can. Travler's current breeding stock is all of basically Parader lines, mostly True Grit, with some Wickmere, Gin Geor, and Enterprise strains.

Both Steve Tehon and Joe Ardizzone are dog photographers who photograph the winners of the Eastern Specialty Shows.

WICKMERE

Wickmere Collies are a family project of Lt. Colonel and Mrs. George H. Roos and their daughter Shelley, who are now located at Manassas, Virginia. As a family with an army career, they have done considerable moving from place to place; thus their Collie breeding has been interrupted at various periods. But the success and fame of their kennel despite this fact, and the fact that they never had any particular goal as their ambition when they started or through the years, makes the extent of their achievements all the more remarkable.

In reminiscing, Bobbee Roos comments that she supposes it is she who started it all, as her interest in animals has been lifelong. Raised in Walla Walla, Washington, there were always horses and cattle around, and a whole series of adopted stray dogs.

Ch. Wickmere Battle Chief, by Ch. Wickmere War Dance x Bonnie Dawn Mac Tavish, from a breeding to Ch. Wickmere Cotillion produced Ch. Shamont Sabrina, the dam of seven champions. Battle Chief is owned by Mrs. George H. Roos, Jr., Wickmere Collies.

It was in 1952 when George and Bobbee Roos appeared at the home of Ben and Isabelle Butler in Richmond, Washington, on a visit which resulted in their acquisition of a five-month-old male puppy who quite a while later became Champion Kinmont's Enchanted Flame. He was a son of Champion Kinmont Kerry ex Star of Arrowhill. The following year, as a birthday present to Bobbee from George, the Butlers shipped out a sable bitch to them in Albuquerque, New Mexico, thus providing Wickmere with its foundation bitch. Her name was Kinmont Kachina and she was a half sister to Flame, being by International Champion Kinmont Sheyne ex Star of Arrowhill. Kachina was from a repeat of the breeding that had produced Arrowhill Ace High, the outstanding sire owned by Florence Cummings.

Then came the order transferring George to England, which necessitated the sale of the dogs. Flame went to Mary Killingsworth

Ch. Wickmere Wedding Bell, winner of six Working Group firsts and Specialties, litter sister to Ch. Wickmere Anniversary Waltz. Owned by Mrs. George H. Roos, Jr., Wickmere Collies.

for whom he completed his championship in 1958. Kachina was leased to friends, to be returned when the tour of duty in England came to an end.

The selection of Wickmere as the kennel name for the Roos Collie activities makes an interesting story. Their interest in the breed continued while they were in England, and they were anxious to acquire a dog or two while there. However, to register a dog in England a kennel name is a necessity, something which they had not really thought about owing to the shortness of time they were "in" Collies while still in New Mexico. The formality in England is that a list of eight names must be submitted to The Kennel Club. The selection, as Bobbee puts it, "ran the gamut from Ron Shell and Shell Ron" (both of these combining the names of their son and daughter, Ron and Shelley) to long forgotten alternates. Then one day during a family outing, they noticed a name which intrigued them; it was on an arrow marking a pathway. It said "Wickmere," and became the name with which the Rooses' kennel name application ended (the eighth)—and it was approved and assigned them. That is how one of the Collie world's most famous names was decided upon!

The first dog to carry it was a young sable, Danvis Digger of Wickmere, who had already won his Junior Warrant for his American owners, quite handily, and was expected to mature into an excellent dog. Then came the transfer back to the States, where the Rooses' new station was in Des Moines, Iowa. Several of Digger's puppies made the trip back with the family, and Digger was to follow. Evidently the party with whom he had been left considered him too excellent to come to the States, and thus refused to ship him.

Once settled in Des Moines the Rooses were eager to return to breeding Collies, but needed some new dogs with which to do so. Kachina, sad to relate, had escaped from her run and was killed on the highway while they were in England. However, they were able to acquire a daughter of hers by Carroll's Cavalcade (a son of International Champion Emeral's My Son O'Duke ex Wee Kirk's Miss Carroll) as a replacement for the loss.

This bitch became Wickmere's Spring Wind. Bred to Champion Arrowhill Oklahoma Redman, she produced Wickmere Honeybun, a litter sister to a bitch who, when bred to Champion Parader's Country Squire, produced Champion Highacre's Valiant for

Lois Smith. Honeybun was bred to Champion Parader's Dark Victory, and produced a litter which included Victory's Paraderette and Parader's Miss America. Paraderette was one of two bitches from the litter purchased by Steve Field, who bred her to Champion Parader's Country Squire by whom she produced Champion Parader's P.Z. Pawnee. Miss America went to Dr. and Mrs. Craft, for whom she produced Champion Crafthaven's Amber.

While attending a meeting of the Iowa Collie Club at the home of Dr. and Mrs. Crosley, the Rooses found their hosts anxious to cut back on the number of their dogs, and therefore were eager to sell a litter sister to Champion Wesbara's Bold Venture (by Champion Parader's Bold Venture ex Brooknelle Honeybear, a Venture daughter), for a very inconsequential price. Leaving no time for the Crosleys to change their minds, George and Bobbee had the bitch in their station wagon and on their way home almost within minutes!

Wesbara Ventura, as the bitch was named, became a strong force in Wickmere pedigrees. By Champion Parader's Lochinvar she produced Wickmere Wynken, a bitch who was kept by the Rooses. At her first show, the Collie Club of America Specialty in Kansas, she won second in her Futurity class under judge Florence Cummings.

When the next transfer came through, George and Bobbee Roos and family wound up in Texas, taking with them only Ventura and Wynken. Honeybun went to Miriam Pittsenberger in Redfield, Iowa. Ventura was sent back to Parader Kennels for breeding to Champion Dark Victory, from which she produced the first Wickmere Whiplash, a most beautiful dog, and a very special favorite with Shelley. His first time in the ring he became 2nd Sweepstakes finalist at the Kansas Specialty. He did quite nicely for himself winning Sweepstakes honors, some major reserves, and a four-point major at the Colorado Specialty prior to the decision being reached that he should sit back and mature awhile. Wynken continued to be shown, winning numerous open classes but then winding up reserve to a beautiful blue bitch.

The Rooses had been noting with admiration the outstanding puppies being sired by Champion Merrie Oaks Midnite Star (Champion Merrie Oaks Star Boarder-Champion Merrie Oaks Julep), so it was decided to breed Wynken to him. This breeding produced Champion Wickmere Reveille, Wickmere's first homebred champion.

The next transfer was to Washington, D.C. Several good youngsters

96

Ch. Wickmere Chimney Sweep pictured winning Best of Breed at Bucks County under judge Ed Sellman. The trophy, given by Christiana Van Dyck, was a silver martini pitcher which had been won by W.R. Van Dyck in 1939 with Ch. Honeybrook Big Parade at Kennel Club of Atlantic City. Howard Van Dyck had found these treasures in the attic following the death of his parents, and donated the shaker which had a silver Collie figure standing on top of the lid. At Devon in 1971 Chimney Sweep also won the large sterling silver bowl offered by Mr. and Mrs. John LaFore at Devon, to be won three times by the same exhibitor for permanent possession, which he had also won the previous two years. How many memories these beautiful trophies bring to mind! Chimney Sweep is handled here by his owner, Mrs. George Roos.

The great Ch. Wickmere Rapunzel winning her third major under judge Benjamin Butler at the Collie Club of Maryland in 1968, handled by owner Mrs. George H. Roos, Jr. The Collie Club of America loving cup was presented by Mrs. Virginia Hampton who was District Director at that time.

were sold as pets and Champion Wickmere Reveille was sent, on lease, to Rhode Island. Christy was left in Texas to be bred to Champion Merrie Oaks Midnite Star. Lash and Wynken accompanied their owners in the station wagon headed for their new home. The Rooses entered into a period of misfortune with the dogs at this point. Whiplash, who had been boarded at a well-recommended kennel as the family was staying in a motel while looking for a house in Washington, was dead when they returned to pick her up. Then Wynken was sent to be bred to Champion Rock Dorbet's Star Parader, developed metritis, and in spite of all efforts to save her life, was lost. Ventura, owing to complications necessitating a Caesarean, lost her entire litter. Suddenly everything was lost. This might have stopped many a less dedicated breeder from trying to continue. Not so, fortunately with Bobbee Roos! A double granddaughter of Wickmere Honeybun was sent on from Miriam Pittsenberger, thus again giving them a line to their original foundation.

The Rooses had the tremendously good fortune of being able to acquire Champion Merrie Oaks Midnite Star on lease from Dick Warren in Texas. He was already the sire of eight champions, including six of those produced from Champion Alteza The Silver Lining. Midnite was named sire of the year in 1965. He himself was from a litter of four champions by Champion Merrie Oaks Star Boarder ex Champion Merrie Oaks Julep. A sister, Champion Merrie Oaks Shooting Star, finished her title by going Best in Show, all-breed, from the classes!

Midnite Star's contributions to Wickmere and to the Collie world were impressive. In addition to Silver Lining's champions by him, there is Champion Regaline's Blue Intuition who is the dam of eight champions, six rough and two smooth. Bred to the Midnite son Champion Wickmere War Dance she produced three champions; then bred to War Dance's son (thus Midnite's grandson), Champion Wickmere Chimney Sweep, she had two more champions. Also there is Champion Wickmere Cotillion, linebred to Midnite, who, bred to Midnite's grandson, Battle Chief, produced Champion Shamont Sabrina, the dam of seven rough champions.

Also involved in the rebuilding of Wickmere were a sable and white bitch, Bellbrooke's Miss Ginger, purchased from the Guilianos, and a bitch who became Wickmere Sun Dance, from Tri Acres Shadowbox bred to Champion Wickmere Reveille.

The memorable bitch who became Champion Wickmere Rapunzel was a stud fee puppy, selected by Bobbee Roos as pick-of-the-litter from a breeding of Bray's Holly of Wickmere (Midnite and Honey). No one agreed with her choice at the time. But history has proven how very correct she had been!

Rapunzel became a Best in Show winner (Alva Rosenberg, who so honored her, lost no time in seeing her quality—typical of Alva's keen and highly respected "dog sense"). She won and placed in numerous Groups, and she had at least several Specialties to her credit. Her final appearance, at age 11 years, was at the Collie Club of America Specialty in Louisville 1978.

Bred back to Wesbara Ventura, his granddam, Champion Wickmere Reveille produced two sable bitches, Wickmere Bewitched and Wickmere Sunkist. Although neither was ever shown, both played important roles in the development of Wickmere's breeding program. Bred to Champion Bellbrooke's Master Pilotson, Bewitched produced Wickmere Royal Guardsman, a beautiful dog who disliked shows. Sunkist was bred to him; then came Wickmere Wendy Wonder, who was the dam of Champion Wickmere Golden Chimes, Best in Sweepstakes, Collie Club of America 1972 and Wickmere Windswept who has made her presence felt in California Collie circles and won Veteran Bitches at the 1981 National.

Reveille bred to Midnite Star produced the tri male, Champion Wickmere War Dance, the first homebred champion for young Shelley Roos.

American and Canadian Wickmere Chimney Sweep, by Champion Wickmere War Dance ex Watts Branch Coventry Lady (daughter of Champion Wickmere Reveille) sired at least 17 champions and stands behind a great many more. He had completed his championship by ten months of age, and was Best of Breed at the Mason and Dixon Collie Club Specialty at 11 months, his first time out as a special. His total record, of which the Rooses never kept an exact count, included Best in Show wins, Group Firsts and placements, Specialty wins, plus Best of Breed at the National in 1972 judged by Steve Field. Sadly, this marvelous dog died at only ten years old.

There have been many other "greats" at Wickmere over the years: Champion Wickmere Battle Chief, by Champion Wickmere War Dance ex Bonnie Dawn MacTavish; Champion Wickmere War Paint, by Wickmere Kaleidoscope ex Wickmere Call Me Madam; Champion Wickmere Wedding Bell, who is one of the leading bitches in Collie history having won the Working Group on six occasions; Wickmere Wedding Veil, who is the dam of several champions in South America where she was exported as a puppy; Champion Wickmere Anniversary, another from the same litter as Bell and Veil; Champion Wickmere Gild The Lily; and quite a goodly number more.

Champion Wickmere Branding Iron was sold to Japan, where he has sired five champions.

Champion Wickmere Silver Bullet was purchased as a birthday gift for Shelley Roos. Although he has not been campaigned to any extent, he has more than made his presence felt as a memorable stud dog. His first champion was Wickmere Tear Drop, from Champion Wickmere Swept in Time. Now a number of champions by this lovely dog are in competition, and will be seen in the pages of this book. He has won the Stud Dog Class at the National on at least two occasions, and there seems little doubt that the number of champions to his credit will continue to steadily increase.

Carnwath Here I Am, bred and owned by Sue Symington, Carnwath Kennels, Toronto, Ontario is a Canadian Champion and major-pointed in the United States. A daughter of Ch. Shamont Stormalong out of the Canadian Best in Show bitch, Am. and Can. Ch. Carnwath Platinum Filigree.

Chapter 5

Collies in Canada

Collies are a well loved breed in Canada, and there is a steady, consistent interest in them. Some splendid dogs appear in competition at the dog shows and the breeders are doing well at producing quality in which to take pride.

On the following pages we describe for you what is taking place in some of the well-known Canadian Collie kennels, and bring you pictures of some very handsome winning dogs.

The Canadian Collie and Shetland Sheepdog Association, Incorporated, whose secretary is Miss Jane Davies, 78 Blvd. St. Jean, Pte. Claire, Quebec, is an active organization furthering the interest of both Collies and Shelties. The same is also true in the case of the Dominion Collie and Shetland Sheepdog Association, Mrs. Marilyn Newstead, Secretary, R.R. 1, Gormley, Ontario LOH IGO.

KAIRLAKE

Kairlake Collies are located at Ile de Chene, Manitoba, in Canada, where Laurrie and Irenne Majcher have been breeding Collies for a number of years. The principal "star" of this establishment is the very handsome Canadian Champion Kairlake Silver Dollar Son, now five years old, who has won a Best in Show, over 30 Group placements, and 100 times Best of Breed. He is a very special dog to his owners, as he was their first homebred champion and their first Best in Show dog—from the very first litter they ever bred!

"Smokey" was picked by Laurrie Majcher when Laurrie was only 15 years old and the puppy only just born. As her mother, Irenne says, "they grew up together," and Laurrie has been the only person ever to have handled "Smokey" in the show ring.

The foundation bitch at Kairlake was Canadian Champion Lickcreek's Classic Rythym, a linebred granddaughter of Champion Lickcreek's Pizzazz, and the breeding program now is concentrating on the Champion Ravette's The Silver Meteor-Pizzazz blend. Mrs. Majcher comments, "I have to take my hat off to Meteor for endowing his offspring with a real love of the show ring and unique personalities and the ability to last."

Kairlake dogs are known for excellence in obedience as well as in the conformation ring.

Silver Dollar Son, as his name implies, is by Champion Shomont Silver Dollar (by the Glen Hill Full Dress son, Champion Ravette's The Silver Meteor) from Ryerlea's Golden Dawn (granddaughter of Champion Sovereign Fife and Drum and Champion Piper Glen's Shanendorn Valley).

NATIONVIEW

Nationview Collies are owned by Wally and Wendy Ace at South Mountain, Ontario. Based primarily on American stock, the kennels are linebreeding, working steadily towards their owner's ideal Collie. The foundation bitch and a blue dog have been heavily influential in creating the Nationview "look." Both of them were purchased from noted American breeders.

Among the Collies owned by the Aces are American and Canadian Champion Mountainblue's Silver Magician, who completed Canadian title at less than nine months old with Best of Breed over specials; then completed championship in the United States with all Specialty majors. Magician is a son of Canadian Champion Nationview's Jewell's Pirate ex Canadian Champion Mountainblue's Touch of Magic.

Canadian Champion Carnwath Nationview Phantomime has made his presence felt in both the United States and Canada. He was bred by Sue Symington, from Jancade Foolish Pleasure ex Canadian Champion Carnwath Lace Tapestry.

Another well-known Damn Yankee kid, Canadian Champion Nationview Double Take, is from Canadian Champion Mountainblue Nationview Effigy. This one is a homebred.

Can. Ch. Nationview Double Take, by Can. and Am. Ch. Twin Creek's Damn Yankee ex Can. Ch. Mountainblue Nationview Effigy, bred and owned by Wendy and Wally Ace, South Mountain, Ontario.

The importance of the role the Damn Yankee line has played in Nationview's development is further proven by two others he has sired. Canadian Champion Nationview Yankee Doodle Dandy completed Canadian title with Best of Breed wins over specials, has United States points gained in keen competition, and was first in the 6-9 months puppy class at the Collie Club of America National Specialty in 1982. Dandy is homebred and from Val Japi Juvenis. This latter combination also produced Canadian Champion Levallon Nationview's Dazzlin', who became a Canadian Champion with two Specialty majors won from the puppy classes.

Canadian Champion Honeybun's Smoke Screen has points in the States and some good Specialty wins in Canada and was bred by Shirley Dowski, by Honeybun's Super Charge ex Honeybun's Blue Non O'Charisma.

SABELIN

Sabelin Collies, breeding sables, tris and blues, are owned by Carol Darnley, Claremont, Ontario, whose dogs have distinguished themselves in both conformation competition and in obedience.

Among the noted winners to be found here are Champion Our Mistymorn's Blue Mist, by Champion Daystorm's Black Lancer from

Ch. Our Mistymorn's Blue Mist, blue merle daughter of Ch. Daystorm's Black Lancer ex Aberdeen's Tumbler, bred by Sheila and Bill Cahill. Owned by Carol Darnley, Claremont, Ontario.

Ch. Our Mistymorn's Blue Mist, *left,* and Ch. Sabelin's Whistlin' Dixie, her ten-month-old puppy along with admiration for their beauty, by Ch. Daystorm's Black Lancer have won Best Brace in Show, on more than one occasion. Owned by Carol Darnley, Claremont, Ontario.

Aberdeen's Tumbler, bred by Sheila and Bill Cahill, born January 11, 1979. This lovely bitch has distinguished herself in several areas, being a well-known winner; one half of a Best in Show winning brace (with her son by Champion Daystorm's Black Lancer, Champion Sabelin's Whistlin' Dixie); and the dam of Champion Sabelin's Knight Rider, C.D., Champion Sabelin's Checkmate, C.D.N./Am. C.D.X., in addition to the aforementioned Champion Sabelin's Whistlin' Dixie.

Champion Sabelin's Seventh Son, C.D.X./Am. C.D., is a beautiful and talented son of Champion Rebel Rouser of Carsaig from Carsaig's Rambling Taffy Ann. He was the No. 3 Obedience Collie for 1982 in the United States, Delaney System, and is a High in Trial Obedience dog.

Champion Mistymorn's Lady Sabelin, C.D., sired by Champion Alfenloch Expression from Mistymorn's Cinnamon Spice has as her grandparents Two Jay's Hanover Enterprise (Parader's Country Squire-Cul-Mor's Highland Holly); Champion Alfenloch A Dream Come True (Tartanside The Gladiator-Lappan's Delightful Countess); Champion Sandpiper's Step Aside (Champion Sandpiper's Superwave-Champion Twin Creek's Dark Tempest); and Daystorm's Misty Dawn (Lappan's Adventurer-Daystorm Buttons'n' Bows).

SCOTCHSKYE

Scotchskye Collies are owned by Sandra and Hugh Campbell at Canning, Nova Scotia, in Canada.

All of the dogs in this kennel are based on the Sovereign bloodlines which were started during the early 1950's by Mrs. Ariel Sleeth, also very famous in the Shetland Sheepdog world. Mrs. Campbell firmly believes in the judicious use of both inbreeding and linebreeding to improve existing qualities. As a result, her dogs are all closely related individuals.

The foundation dog at Scotchskye is the handsome Champion Ryerlea's Evening Breeze, now past ten years old.

TRICOUNTY

Tricounty Collies belong to Brian and Hazel Hampson, Jarvis, Ontario, Canada.

The very aptly named Canadian Champion Pebblebrook's Star at Tricounty is a dog in whom the Hampsons justly take pride. He is by American and Canadian Champion Twin Creek's Damn Yankee ex Canadian Champion Pebblebrook Supersweet, his pedigree tracing back to American and Canadian Champion Carnwath's Evergreen (winner of the Collie Club of America Specialty in 1981) of whom he is a grandson and American Champion Twin Creek's True Grit of whom he is a great-grandson.

"Riley," as Star is known to friends and family, was bred by Dieter and Marion Liebsch. He completed his championship in Canada at age nine months in just three shows, and on his first showing in the

This irresistible baby Collie is Pebblebrook Dream at Tricounty. "Tiffany" was sired by Am. and Can. Ch. Pebblebrook Damn Yankee ex Twin Creek's Elusive Dream. Owned by Brian and Hazel Hampson, Tricounty Collies, Ontario.

United States, at 12 months, was Best of Breed at Saginaw Valley for his first American points. Since then he has been through the process of growing a new coat for his return to the show ring as a mature dog.

Also sired by American and Canadian Champion Twin Creeks Damn Yankee is the well-known bitch, Canadian Champion Tricounty's Rambling Rose, who is from Champion Lamours Midnight Fantasy, a granddaughter of American and Canadian Champion Tartanside Heir Apparent and from a daughter of Champion Lamours Major and Champion Campsieviews Connie. This bitch, known as "Annie," is a homebred who completed her Canadian title at age 12 months with three 5-point majors. In the States, she won her first major at ten months going Best of Winners under Mrs. Helen Miller Fisher. She is a tri-factored sable.

Pelido Black Prince is by Brettonpark Highlander of Dunsinane ex Pelido Doretta of Dunsinane. Sire of champions in all three colors: namely, Ch. Pelido Spartacus, Ch. Pelido Black Belle, and Ch. Chambrae Polar Moon at Pelido. Owned and bred by Mr. and Mrs. P. W. Burtenshaw, Godalming, Surrey, England.

Chapter 6

Collies in Great Britain

Collies are a breed that has remained consistently popular and of good type and quality in Great Britain. Both the Roughs and the Smooths are admired and appreciated in show competition, making notable wins.

The following kennel stories will bring you up-to-date on some of those dogs and people currently in the Collie limelight in this part of the world. British Collies have been exported to many countries over the years, and have formed the foundation of numerous famous strains. From the very beginning, Collie breeders in Great Britain have done their jobs well, the result being seen wherever Collies are known and loved.

LAUREATS

Laureats Kennels feature Smooth Collies and their owner, Mrs. Y. Gillibrand, Gorton, Manchester, England, is a highly successful breeder of them.

Among the dogs at this kennel are to be found Foxearth Lord Fountleroy at Laureats, who is a well-known winner at Championship Shows, has numerous Best Puppy awards to his credit, along with wins in Novice, Junior and Post Graduate Classes even before reaching ten months old. He was sired by English Champion Astrellita The Silversmith (grandson of Champion Treewood Black King and Champion Dancerwood Freelance) from Foxearth Frappant (a Champion Jalonda's Jacanapes daughter and a granddaughter of Champion Chicnoir Midnight Sultan and Champion Peterblue Nigel).

Limelight at Laureats and La Di Da of Laureats at Manchester Championship show with their owner's grandson. Owned by Mrs. Y. Gillibrand, Gorton, Manchester, England.

Cownbred Trisatin at Laureats has been shown somewhat sparingly but made good wins at Championship and Open Shows. She was Best Smooth Collie in Show at the Lancashire and Cheshire Collie Club Open Show in January 1984, and has recently raised a litter by Limelight at Laureats. Trisatin is by Jaunty Johnny of Juberes at Bothways (grandson of Champion Ramsey of Rokeby and Champion Brettonpark Vanity Fair) from Queen of Pulson at Garbosa (granddaughter of Champion Astrellita The Silversmith and Champion Dancerwood Bewitched of Astrellita).

La-Di-Da at Laureats is a tri-color dog by English Champion Foxearth Winnings The Game at Bothways (Champion Foxearth Gold Fever-International and World Champion Jubilate at Mallicot) from Beechwyre Blue Bonnet, the latter a granddaughter of Champion Grancoats Blue Destiny and Champion Goldcrest Midnight Velvet. This royally bred young dog was winner of Best Dog Puppy at Manchester Championship show, and he is having additional exciting victories at all types of shows.

Limelight at Laureate was a Rescue Dog who at the time of this writing has been with Mrs. Gillibrand for about three months. She has been showing him with notable success, his wins including Best Collie, both coats, and Best Working Dog in Show. He was born in 1982, and is by English Champion Chicnor Midnight Sultan from Sylbecq Show In Harvest at Lilymead (Champion Foxearth Gold Fever-Champion Sylbecca Fleur De Lys).

PELIDO

Pelido Collies are owned by Mr. and Mrs. P.W. Burtenshaw, at Godalming, England, breeders who have surely made a significant contribution to Collie quality and beauty through their many correct and handsome dogs.

The first champion dog owned by the Burtenshaws was the stunning Champion Pelido Copper Beech. Copper Beech won three Challenge Certificates and twice was Best in Show at Collie Club Specialties. He was homebred by the Burtenshaws, and as a producer, he became the sire of Champion Pelido Angel Fingers, the first champion bitch at Pelido.

Angel Fingers has won three Challenge Certificates, a Junior Warrant, one Best Puppy in Show All-breeds, five times Best in Show at Collie Club Specialties. She is the granddam to Champion Pelido Black Belle, also owner-bred by Mr. and Mrs. Burtenshaw.

A winner of very special prominence at this kennel is Champion Cathanbrae Polar Moon at Pelido. With seven Challenge Certificates and four Reserve Challenge Certificates, the other honors awarded this Collie include twice Best in Show at Collie Club Specialties. As a sire he has distinguished himself by producing two Rough and one Smooth champion, along with an eight-month-old daughter with a Junior Warrant and a Challenge Certificate in England. Polar Moon's influence has also been felt on the Continent where two Rough and one Smooth champions carry the banner for him and for his breeders.

Another homebred, Champion Pelido Black Belle, has attained three Challenge Certificates, three reserve Challenge Certificates, and Best in Show honors at both all-breed events and Collie Specialties.

Champion Pelido Silver Lady, also a homebred, gained her title in only five shows, winning her own three Challenge Certificates but "standing in the wings" while her kennel mates took the dog cer-

Eng. Ch. Cathanbrae Polar Moon at Pelido, by Pelido Black Prince ex Cathanbrae Southern Belle, bred by Mrs. T. Taylor. Owned by Mr. and Mrs. P. W. Burtenshaw, Pelido Collies.

tificates at the other two. She was Best of Breed at the British Collie Club and the Midland Collie Club Championship Shows.

It is easy to see that the majority of the Pelido champions have been homebred. Among the exceptions to this have been Champion Jaden Mister Blue at Pelido, winner of three Challenge Certificates, three Reserves, Best in Show at a Collie Club Specialty, and Best Puppy in Show all-breeds. Bred by Mr. and Mrs. Gooden, Mister Blue descends from the family nonetheless, being a grandson of Polar Moon on both sides.

Then there is Champion Jeffield Esquire, bred and owned by Mrs. Doreen Field, who before her unexpected death had already won a Challenge Certificate with him under Mrs. Burtenshaw. Obviously an admirer of Esquire, Mrs. Burtenshaw added him to her own Collie family, won a fourth Challenge Certificate with him at Crufts in 1983, and is now enjoying watching the progress of his Challenge Certificate-winning son.

Among the distinguished homebreds belonging to the Burtenshaws is Champion Pelido Spartacus, himself a Best in Show winner at an important Collie Club Specialty, and with three Challenge Certificates and eight Reserve Certificates on his own record, the Burtenshaws point with pride to the fact that he has sired Best in Show winners at both Collie Club and all breed events, and that his progeny also include other Challenge Certificates and Reserve Challenge Certificate winners.

Mr. and Mrs. Burtenshaw stand very high in the ranks of Collie breeders around the world. They were the top Collie breeders in

Ch. Pelido Copper Beech is by Leecroft Lover Boy of Dunsinane ex Pelido Hunnycombe Saffron. This sire of Ch. Pelido Angel Fingers is owned and was bred by Mr. and Mrs. P. W. Burtenshaw, Pelido Collies.

Ch. Jeffield Esquire, by Ch. Little Caesar at Corydon ex Shanbe Stroll Awhile at Jeffield was bred by the late Mrs. Field. Now owned by Mr. and Mrs. P. W. Burtonshaw, Esquire won his fourth Challenge Certificate at Crufts in 1983.

Opposite page: *(Top)* Eng. Ch. Pelido Silver Lady, by Ch. Cathambrae Polar Moon at Pelido ex Pelido Minuetto Allegretto, owned and bred by Mr.and Mrs. P. W. Burtenshaw. *(Bottom)* Pelido Double Fantasy, by Ch. Arranbrook Mr. Chips of Aberhill ex Pelido French Knickers, at 13 months. Owned and bred by Mrs. P. W. Burtenshaw, Pelido Collies.

Eng. Ch. Pelido Spartacus, by Pelido Black Prince ex Brettonpark Golden Dream at Pelido, owned and bred by Mr. and Mrs. P. W. Burtenshaw.

England for 1982; the Top Winners that same year, and won the dog Challenge Certificate at Crufts in 1983. Looking at the photos of their dogs, it is easy to foresee many more of the same in the future for these dedicated fanciers.

RIFFLESEA

Rifflesea Collies are owned by Mrs. H.R. Hunt at Portshead, Avon, England. Mrs. Hunt, formerly Hazel Collins, trained at the Bristol Old Vic and worked as an actress until her marriage to Dr. K.G. Collins broke up in 1948. During this period she raised four children and helped to run her then-husband's medical practice. Afterwards, she returned to school, earned an Honours Degree in Law, and worked as a litigation lawyer until her re-marriage. Now, since becoming Mrs. Hunt, she is able to spend more time with her beloved Collies, the breed she has owned since purchasing her first in 1943.

This earliest Collie came from Mrs. George's famous Beulah Kennels, and was bred by her new owner to Beulah's Night Victorious, who was a litter brother to the famed U.S.A. Champion Beulah's Silver Don Mario of St. Adrian's. In this litter she produced a tri bitch for Mrs. Hunt called Beulah's Night Flare who, in her turn, was mated to a merle son of English and American Champion Eden Diadam. The sole surviving puppy of this litter was Lilac of Ladypark who produced several champions for Miss Grey of Ladypark Collies.

Mrs. Hunt purchased from Miss Grey two puppies who both became champions: Champion Lad of Ladypark (brother to Champion Lochinvar) and Lochinvar's daughter, Champion Rose of Ladypark. From these two came the well-known trio, Champion Rifflesea Resplendence, Champion Rifflesea Regality, and Champion Rifflesea Reward. They provided foundation breeding stock for several highly successful Collie kennels of the present day.

Beulah's Night Flare, for her second litter, was bred to Mrs. Hunt's Champion Lad of Ladypark and in this litter produced the tri, Rifflesea Royalist, who became sire of the immortal Champion Westcarrs Blue Minoru as well as several other champions. Mrs. Hunt notes that

Rifflesea Restraint, winner of Challenge Certificates and Reserve Challenge Certificates is another of the outstanding Collies owned by the noted breed authority Mrs. H. R. Hunt, Rifflesea Kennels, Portishead, Avon, England.

Sandiacre Snow Pearl of Rifflesea, winner of Challenge Certificates and Reserve Challenge Certificates, by the Challenge Certificate winning Sandiacre Softly Softly ex Ch. Sandiacre Seed Pearl. Owned by Mrs. H. R. Hunt, Rifflesea Collies, Portishead, Avon, England.

"it has been calculated that every merle Collie in England today can trace pedigree back to Royalist."

Now in the mid-1980's, Mrs. Hunt still has Collies in the kennel, although the number now is mostly limited to the old dogs. Mrs. Hunt has become an extremely popular judge, whose other Collie-involved activities include running a magazine on the breed and the present project of writing a book on Rough, Smooth, and Border Collies.

During a judging engagement in Italy last year (1984), Mrs. Hunt awarded Best in Show to a Collie who impressed her tremendously, then Italian Champion Incredibly Blu di Cambiane. So admiring was

Coleanne Dark Star of Pepperstone, born April 1982, by Krisendale Country-man of Aberhill ex Albrett Star Attention at Coleanne. This tri-colored bitch owned by V. A. R. Vanstone, The Paddock Kennels, Sittingbourne, England.

she of this exquisite dog that she persuaded his owner, Mrs. Garabelli, to send him over to England for a visit. He became a champion there four months after coming out of quarantine, and it was Mrs. Hunt who had the pleasure of showing him. It was hoped that the opportunity of using this dog at stud while there will prove to have been highly beneficial to the British Collie in coming generations! He is descended from American Champion Knightwood Rip Tide, combined with the finest English blue merle breeding. As we write he, Incredibly Blu, is now in Sweden to become a Scandinavian Champion prior to returning to his home in Italy.

This was a famous early Collie exported from Great Britain to Australia. Ormskirk Amazement was a son of a noted producing bitch Sweet Lassie.

Aust. Ch. Fairloch Ben Lomond, by Aust. Ch. Fairloch Major Dundee ex Aust. Ch. Fairloch Night Fame owned by Doteon Kennels, Eon and Dorothy Densworth, Queanbeyan, New South Wales.

Chapter 7

Collies in Australia

Through recent years the rapport between dog show enthusiasts in Australia and their counterparts in the United States has grown at a steady pace. There has been an impressive number of judges traveling back and forth between the two countries fulfilling judging assignments; and thus we have learned much about each other and each other's dogs.

All we have learned on the subject fills us with admiration for these people and their determination to not only own but to breed superior animals. They have obviously done their homework well in Australia, purchasing leading bloodlines from England and the United States where needed, to work into their breeding programs, then using these purchases to best advantage. Considering the long and arduous quarantine involved in bringing dogs to Australia, tremendous credit is due them for their perseverance.

Rough Collies are tremendously popular with the Australians, turning out impressive entries and accounting for important winning at the prestige shows. As an example, during 1984 alone there were 110 at the Sydney Royal Easter Show; 132 (the largest individual entry in any breed there) at the Adelaide Royal; and 132 at the Melbourne Royal, with its huge entry of 6,731, made Rough Collies the second largest entry. The Sydney Spring Fair drew 113 in this breed.

Not only are the entries of good size, but Collie winning is spectacular. For instance, the Best in Show at the Brisbane Royal in August 1984 was won by the sable Champion Braeden Show

Dancer, breeder-owned, handled by the popular all-rounder judge Miss Glenys Acreman, in a total entry of more than 3,000 dogs.

Another notable win was that of the Working Group at the Sydney Royal Easter Show by the lovely Glenskye Miss Mindy.

The following kennel resumes from Australia give you an idea of the quality dogs in competition there, and of the impact they have had as winners.

DOTEON

Doteon Collies at Queanbryan, New South Wales, in Australia are owned by Eon and Dorothy Densworth and have some beautiful, prestigious winning Collies to their credit.

Australian Champion Fairloch Spartacus was born September 17, 1974, bred by Fairloch Kennels. When he retired from the show ring he had been Best Exhibit in Show All Breeds on 15 occasions, runner- up to this award many times, 37 times Best Exhibit in the Working Group. During his seven years of campaigning in the show ring, he amassed a total of 2,000 Challenge points, making him one of the most important winning Rough Collies in Australia.

Spartacus's wins included notable ones at the important Royal Shows. He is by Fairloch Fair Viking from Fairloch Forever Amber.

The Densworths also own Australian Champion Fairloch Ben Lomond. This multiple Best in Show and Group winner is now six years old as we write, still going strong and continuing his winning ways.

EINAR

Einar Kennels are owned by Bill and Joan Ranie, Kaleen, A.C.T., Australia, who currently are showing two especially notable young Collies.

Australian Champion Einar Chandelier Blue, a homebred blue merle bitch, has to her credit 11 Best Exhibit in Group awards, under Australian and international judges; eleven runners-up to Best Exhibit in Group awards; two Best Exhibit in Show, all-breeds, awards; and three runners-up to Best Exhibit in Show. Also on three occasions she has been runner up to Best in Specialty.

Aust. Ch. Fairloch Spartacus, by Fairlock Fair Viking ex Fairloch Forever Amber, noted winner owned by Doteon Kennels, Eon and Dorothy Densworth, Queanbeyan, New South Wales, Australia.

This beautiful blue bitch has earned almost 900 Challenge Points in just three and a half years of show competition. Runner-up to Best of Breed at the 1983 RASKC Spring Fair under judge Robert S. Forsyth is one of her recent successes.

Chandelier Blue was born March 10, 1980 by Australian Champion Fairloch Performer ex Australian Champion Milbalind Blue Mandy.

Australian Champion Einar Blue Dynasty is also homebred, and was born November 30, 1982. He has won Best in Exhibit in Group four times, including under Swedish judge Mr. I. Swedrup, which gave him his final points for Australian Championship at but seventeen months of age. He has numerous other in

Show and in Group awards, and considering his youth, should have a bright career still ahead of him. He is by Fairloch Flashback ex Australian Champion Milbalind Blue Mandy.

Then there is the puppy, Einar Blue Tradition, whose development the Ranies are watching with interest. Born November 14, 1983, he is still in Baby Puppy Class as we write, making his presence strongly felt as in ten shows he has won 1st Place on seven occasions and 2nd on the other three. Also he has twice been awarded Best Baby in the Working Group.

Blue Tradition is by Fairloch Performer ex Australian Champion Milbalind Blue Mandy.

HYLINDEN

Hylinden Collies are owned by Mrs. J. Bruce at Mittagong, New South Wales, Australia, who has been a Collie fancier and breeder since the 1960's.

Ch. Hylinden Honeybrook, by Aust. Ch. Glentracy Hylinden Lea ex Hylinden Lady Luck, at four years of age, December 1970. Twice Best of Breed at Sydney Royal and Best Bitch in Working Group. Dam of Aust. Ch. Hylinden Hanky Panky and Ch. Hylinden Hard and Fast. Owned by Mrs. J. Bruce, Mittagong, New South Wales.

Aust. Ch. Hylinden Hotline by Aust. Ch. Hylinden Sapper ex Aust. Ch. Hylinden High Society, at nine months. Sydney's Top Winning Collie for several years. Multiple Best in Show and Group winner. Best of Breed at Sydney Royal and Sydney Spring Show.

There are numerous exciting "stars" among the Collies at Mrs. Bruce's kennel. Champion Hylinden Sapper, by Hylinden Here's Hoping ex Champion Hylinden Hi Fi has won Best of Breed at the Sydney Spring Show (Australia's second largest dog show), and Reserve Champion at the Sydney Royal, which is the biggest show in Australia. This splendid dog has sired 11 champions, including Champion Hylinden Hotline (from Champion Hylinden Hi Society). Hotline has been Sydney's Top Winning Collie for several years during the early 1980's, and her important wins have included Best of Breed at the Sydney Royal and Best of Breed at the Sydney Spring Show. She is the dam of Champion Hylinden Shady Lady.

An especially important dog at Hylinden has been the great Champion Glentracy Hylinden Lea (Hylinden Hallmark-Myone

Aust. Ch. Hylinden Sapper owned by Mrs. J. Bruce, Hylinden Collies, Mittagong, New South Wales.

Bo Peep), who has sired the impressive total of 17 champions. Lea himself twice won Best of Breed at the Sydney Royal, and in 1971 was Challenge Dog as well as sire of the Challenge Bitch and Reserve Challenge Bitch.

Champion Hylinden Honeybrook, a Lea daughter from Hylinden Lady Luck, twice was Best of Breed at Sydney Royal, also Best Bitch in the Working Group under an American judge. She is also an excellent producer, being the dam of Champion Hylinden Hanky Panky and Champion Hylinden Hard and Fast.

Another Best in Show and in Group winner at this kennel is Champion Hylinden Happy Ways, by Champion Hylinden Sapper from Hylinden Happy Days. He is the sire of Champion Hylinden Happy News, and is himself a Best in Show and Best in Group winner.

← **Overleaf:**

Am. and Can. Ch. Akirene's Counter Force, by Ch. Glenecho Set the Style ex Can. Ch. Berridale Akirene Misty Morn, is a multiple all-breed Best in Show, Specialty Best in Show, and Group winner. Owned by Richard and Marjorie Norstrom, Honolulu, Hawaii. Shown by George Schlinker.

1. Windfall's Wonder Woman, U.D., by Ch. Hill Crest Windfall ex Highland's Copper Penny, C.D.X., is another of Bernice Terry's outstanding obedience performers.

2. Ch. Barrett's Mr. J. R. owned by James and Joan Barrett, Jaybar Collies, Pickering, Ohio. The first champion owned by this kennel, Mr. J. R. is a Specialty Best of Breed winner with many other honors to his credit.

3. Shown here is Canadian Ch. Glen Hill Forerunner, litter brother to American Ch. Glen Hill Flash. Both are owned by Helen Williamson and Patricia Starkweather.

4. Aust. Ch. Hylinden Happy Ways, by Ch. Hylinden Sapper ex Hylinden Happy Days, a Best in Show winner and sire of Aust. Ch. Hylinden Happy News. Hylinden Collies, Mrs. J. Bruce, Mittagong, New South Wales, Australia.

5. Pebblebrook Dream At Tricounty, three-month-old puppy by Am. Ch. Twin Creek's Damn Yankee ex Twin Creek's Elusive Dream, bred by Dieter and Marion Liebsch. Owners Brian and Hazel Hampson, Tricounty Collies, Jarvis, Ontario, Canada.

6. Ch. Hampton The Dazzling Heiress, born August 1965, is the daughter of Ch. Debhill Razzle Dazzle ex Ch. Hampton Honor Guard's Heiress. Bred, owned, and handled by Virginia Hampton, Doylestown, Pennsylvania.

131

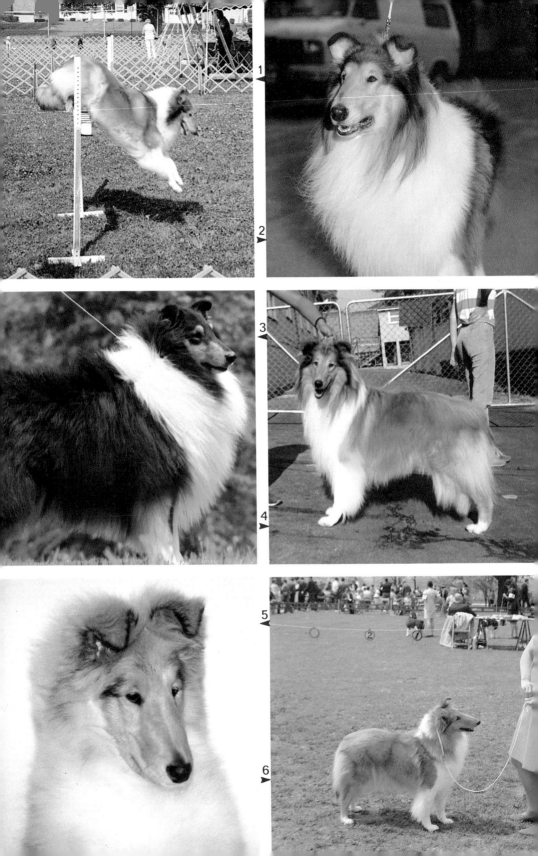

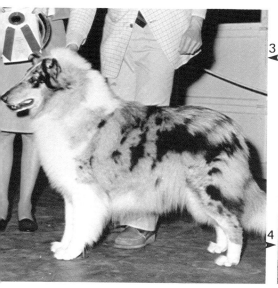

HERDING GROUP
THIRD
OAK RIDGE
KENNEL CLUB SHOW
MAY 1984
PHOTOS BY ALVERSON

← **Overleaf:**

1. Ch. Shamont Silver Dollar, the sire of Ch. Fairlake Silver Dollar Son, is by Ch. Ravette's The Silver Meteor ex Ch. Wickmere Cotillion.

2. Barrett's Forever'N Blue Jeans taking Reserve Winners Bitch at Dan Emmett Kennel Club 1984. Owned by Jaybar Collies, James and Joan Barrett, Pickerington, Ohio.

3. Am. and Can. Ch. Elegy In Blue, by Ch. Gingeor's Indelible Choice ex Bonnie Blue's Columbine, bred by W. and S. Brown. Owner, Linda Goldfarb, Ballston Spa, New York. A foundation bitch at Elegy Collies, Bonnie is behind numerous champions and point winners.

4. Ch. Stoneybrook Silver Saint, C.D., bred by Betsy C. Winberry, owned by Kathy Moll and Mrs. Richmond Fairbanks, here as a youngster is taking Reserve Winners at the Collie Club of America Specialty in 1982.

5. Ch. Canebrake Lucky Lady winning Best of Variety. Handled by Jon Woodring for Kathy Moll, Mildred Burnett and Mrs. Richmond Fairbanks.

6. Ch. Azalea Hill's Canebrake Cameo, tri-color multiple Group and Specialty winner, here is taking Group 3rd after defeating four male specials in the breed at Oakridge Kennel Club. Wade Burns handled for owner, Mrs. Richmond Fairbanks, Greenville, South Carolina.

Overleaf: →

1. Ch. Lisara's One and Only, by Ch. Lisara's Merrytime Drambuie ex Lisara's Bristol Cream, is a highly successful winning Smooth Collie owned by Candy Ardizzone and breeder Carmen Leonard. A multiple Best of Variety winner including Collie Club of Central New York, Mason-Dixon Collie Club, North Country Kennel Club, Albany Kennel Club, Wyoming Valley Kennel Club, and numerous others.

2. Alliance's Wonder Whirl (by Ch. Chris Mik's Jim Beam ex Edenrock Diamond In The Ruff) and Silcrest Xtriordinaire (by Ch. Wickmere Silver Bullet ex Silcrest Sylver Myst) pictured after completing their C.D. Degrees in Obedience. Now working in open towards their next degree. Marlene R. Nicholson, owner, Hendersonville, Tennessee.

1 ▲

2 ▼

BEST OF BREED
OR VARIETY
SAGINAW VALLEY
KENNEL CLUB
SEPT.
1983 BOOTH PHOTO

1▲   2▼

BEST OF
BREED

← **Overleaf:**

1. Can. Ch. Pebblebrook's Star at Tricounty, by Am. and Can. Ch. Twin Creeks Damn Yankee ex Can. Ch. Pebblebrook Supersweet, winning Best of Breed at Saginaw County Kennel Club, Michigan, Sept. 1983. Breeders Dieter and Marion Liebsch. Owners, Brian and Hazel Hampson, Tricounty Collies, Jarvis, Ontario, Canada.

2. Ch. Azalea Hill's Mr. Christopher winning the Collie Club of Indiana Specialty, Bertha Garrison handling for owner Mrs. Richmond Fairbanks, Greenville, South Carolina.

138

Overleaf: →

1. Ch. Elegy Drumbeat, C.D., by Can. Ch. Elegy Distant Drummer ex Kingsbridge Chablis, bred by Linda Goldfarb and Judith Sliwinski. Owned by Linda Goldfarb, Elegy Kennels, Ballston Spa, New York.

2. Ch. Hi-Crest Knock On Wood, by Ch. Ledgedale Money Broker ex Hi-Crest Summer Sprite, was Winners Dog and Best of Winners at the Collie Club of America Specialty in 1982. Joseph Reno, breeder-owner, Hi-Crest Collies, Carteret, New Jersey. Steve Barger handling.

3. Ch. Sedgewyck Lone Survivor, Top Smooth Collie for 1983, was bred by Larry and Diana Goldberg and is owned by Florence D. Shepperd and Diana Goldberg. Ninty-three times Best of Variety, this excellent Smooth Collie had five Group placements in 1983 and seven Group placements in 1984, was Best of Variety at Westminster 1984 and first in the Herding Group at Penn Treaty '84.

4. Travler's Never On A Sundae, taking Best of Opposite Sex at Genesee Valley Kennel Club 1981. Littermate to Travler's Sundae's Child, also pointed, by Ch. Tamarack Asterisk ex Travler's The Sundae Kin (12 points). Bred and owned by Rebecca L. Tehon, Clay, New York.

139

1

2

3

4

Ace

Ace

← **Overleaf:**

1. Ch. Misty Morn's Lady Sabelin, C.D., by Ch. Alfenloch Expression ex Misty Morn's Cinnamon Spice, was bred by Frank McKeown and is owned by Linda McKee and Carol Barnley, Claremont, Ontario. Born May 1979.

2. Can. Ch. Levallon Nationview's Dazzlin' is by Can. and Am. Ch. Twin Creek's Damn Yankee ex Val Japi Juvenis. Breeder, Wendy and Wally Ace and J. Pepin. Owned by the Aces, Nationview Collies, South Mountain, Ontario, Canada.

3. Can. Ch. Carnwath Nationview Pantomime, by Jancada Foolish Pleasure ex Can. Ch. Carnwath Lace Tapestry, bred by Sue Symington. Owners, Wendy and Wally Ace, Nationview Collies, South Mountain, Ontario, Canada. This lovely bitch is a major Specialty reserve winner in the United States.

4. Ch. Elegy Drumbeat, C.D. owned by Linda Goldfarb, Ballston Spa, New York.

Overleaf: →

1. Italian Ch. Lyndale Blue Bayou at Pelido, by Eng. Ch. Cathanbrae Polar Moon at Pelido ex Leanor Hawaiian Princess of Lyndale, owned by Mr. G. Catalano.

2. Ch. SumerHill Inherit The Wind, by Ch. Glenecho Set The Style ex Ch. SumerHill The Winds of Chance, bred by Joan Meagher and owned by Richard and Marjorie Norstrom, Honolulu, Hawaii. A noted Smooth Collie, multiple Group winner.

1▲   2▼

1▲   2▼

← **Overleaf:**

1. Ch. Windarla's World Seeker, by Ch. Windarla's Worldly Wise ex Windarla Presents the Blues, in a photo by Earl Graham. Owners, Ewing and Marlene Nicholson, Hendersonville, Tennessee. Breeders, Arlene and Luwinda Webb. America's No. 1 Collie All Systems, 1981, 1982, and 1983.

2. Ch. Windarla's World Seeker at home in summer coat and enjoying his semi-retirement. Marlene R. Nicholson, owner, Hendersonville, Tennessee.

Overleaf: →

1. Ch. Windarla's Worldly Wise, son of Ch. Wickmere Chimney Sweep, was 1975's No. 12 Collie in Hawkins System. Here shown winning a Working Group. Owned by Marlene Nicholson and handled by Sherri Schmidt.

2. Can. Ch. Sabelin's Seventh Son, C.D.X., Am. C.D., by Ch. Rebel Rouser of Carsaig (Ch. Nansue's Nimrod ex Ch. Lappan's Dots and Dashes) ex Carsaig's Rambling Taffy Ann (Santa Ann's Midas Touch O'Lappan ex Lappan's Dancing Shoes, C.D.) was the No. 3 Obedience Collie in the United States for 1982 (Delaney System) with wins including a High In Trial at the Western Reserve Kennel Club Dog Show with more than 100 obedience entries. Born March 1977. Bred and owned by Carol Darnley, Keswick, Ontario, Canada.

3. Ch. Azalea Hill's Flair pictured going Best of Opposite Sex at the Collie Club of Alabama Specialty in 1981, handled by breeder-owner Mrs. Richmond Fairbanks.

4. Ch. Lisara's Scheherazade, by Ch. Lisara's Merrytime Drambuie ex Tawny Miss of Glenayre, born in 1973, was the No. 1 Smooth Collie, Hawkins System, for 1975. Winner of two Bests in Specialty Show. Bred and owned by Lawrence and Carmen Leonard, Rockwell, Texas.

5. Ch. Elegy Disco Drummer, by Ch. Elegy Drumbeat, C.D. ex Elegy Charisma of Coal Hill, owned by Linda Goldfarb, co-breeder with Mary Stedman. Completed championship as a yearling with a Best of Breed from the classes at a four-point major Specialty and Best of Winners at a five-point major. Sire of winners in his first litter.

6. Ch. Kairlake Silver Dollar Son, by Ch. Shamont Silver Dollar ex Ryerlea's Golden Dawn, born May 1979, owned by Laurrie and Irenne Majcher, Winnipeg, Manitoba, Canada.

147

← **Overleaf:**

1. Ch. Westwend's Fascination, by Ch. Twin Creek's Post Script ex Myriah's Westwend, bred by Sue and Carol Fabeck. Owned by Linda Goldfarb, Elegy Collies, Ballston Spa, New York. Here taking Best of Winners, Trenton Kennel Club 1984.

2. A handsome puppy matured into a most excellent dog! At five years of age, Ch. White Cloud's Bewitch'n Harvest winning a Herding Group for Linda De EuLis and Carmen Leonard, Rockwell, Texas.

3. Ch. Barksdale Early Light, a lovely blue bitch who finished as a puppy, was transferred into specials and then won Best of Opposite Sex to Best of Breed at the 1981 Collie Club of America Specialty. She is another from the litter of four champions by Ch. Wickmere Silver Bullet ex Ch. Highefields Debutante, from Nancy McDonald and Mary Fields.

4. Clendon Brook's Mountain Mist, pointed daughter of Elegy The Student Prince and Elegy Hello Sunshine, bred by Linda Goldfarb, Elegy Collies. Owned by Christine Stewart, Glen Falls, New York.

5. Can. Ch. Nationview Yankee Doodle Dandy, by Can. and Am. Ch. Twin Creek's Damn Yankee ex Val Japi Juvenis, bred and owned by Wendy and Wally Ace, South Mountain, Ontario, Canada.

6. Travler's Sundae's Child, littermate to Travler's Never On A Sundae, homebred owned by Rebecca L. Tehon, Clay, New York.

Overleaf: →

1. Pelido Bolero, by Pelido Double Fantasy ex Pelido Poppy, at ten months of age. Bred by Mr. and Mrs. P. W. Burtonshaw, this is one of many outstanding Collies owned by Mr. G. Catalano in Rome, Italy.

2. The Family: *Seated,* tri-color Ch. Ryerlea's Evening Breeze (sire), by Ch. Glengloamin Blue of Ryerlea ex Sovereign Scotch Twist, and Scotchskye's Gold Sheena (dam) by Ch. Ryerlea's Evening Breeze ex Ryerlea's Honey Buff of Scotchskye. *Lying down,* Scotchskye's Golden Joy, the daughter of Evening Breeze and Gold Sheena. Bred by Sandra Campbell, co-owner with Hugh Campbell, Scotchskye Kennels, Nova Scotia, Canada.

151

← **Overleaf:**

1. Ch. Impromptú Banner Still Waves, by Ch. Clairion's Light Up The Sky ex Impromptú Devil's Delight, was Winners Dog at the National Speciality in 1984. Bred, owned, and handled by Barbara Schwartz, Hollis, New Hampshire.

2. A magnificent group of Pelido Champions owned by Mr. and Mrs. P. W. Burtonshaw, Godalming, Surrey, England. *Left to right:* Eng. Ch. Jeffield Esquire, Eng. Ch. Pelido Black Belle, Eng. Ch. Cathanbrae Polar Moon at Pelido, Eng. Ch. Pelido Sparticus, Eng. Ch. Pelido Angel Fingers, Eng. Ch. Pelido Silver Lady, and Eng. Ch. Jaden Mister Blue at Pelido.

1. Ch. Travler's Flim Flam Man, by Ch. Gin Geor Jack of Tamarack ex River'Odes Bonnie Gay Lady, 1st Open Sable Dogs, Collie Club of America 1977; 1st Veteran Dogs and oldest dog in show, Collie Club of America 1982. Bred and owned by Stephen W. Tehon.

2. Am. and Can. Ch. Akirene's Counter Force, by Ch. Glenecho Set The Style ex Can. Ch. Berridale Akirene Misty Morn, is a Group and Best in Show winner. Breeder, Aki Oishi, owners, Richard and Marjorie S. Norstrom, Honolulu, Hawaii.

3. Ch. Windarla's World Seeker, blue merle Rough Collie, two days before his second birthday here is winning Best in Show from judge Phil Marsh. George Schlinker handles this great dog for owners Marlene and Ewing Nicholson, Hendersonville, Tennessee.

4. Ch. Impromptu Kudos, by Ch. Brandwyne Bayberry Mr. ex Ch. Impromptu Repartee, finished in 1974. Bred and owned by Barbara Schwartz, Impromptu Collies, Hollis, New Hampshire.

← **Overleaf:**

1. Waiting to go in the ring, Candray-Woodwind's Sprinkles, C.D.X. (Ch. Candray Concorde ex Ch. Hi-Vu Silver Siren) bred by Jan and George Wanamaker, owned by Bernice Terry, Endwell, New York.

2. Nationview's Fancy Pants, C.D., by Can. and Am. Ch. Tartanside Heir Apparent ex Honeybun's Dunroamin, owned by Shari Pettigrew and Wendy and Wally Ace.

3. Ch. Elegy Brigadoon, by Ch. Witchaway's Rhythm An Blues ex Elegy The Contralto, was bred and is owned by Linda Goldfarb, Ballston Spa, New York.

4. This lovely and highly promising puppy by Ch. Stoneybrook Silver Saint, C.D. ex Lizdon's Merry Frolicker, is Deep River Blue Satin Slippers. Owned by Kathy V. Moll, this youngster won reserve to a four-point major her first time at the point shows at six months of age.

158

Eng. Ch. Jeffield Esquire, by Ch. Little Caesar at Corydon ex Shanbe Stroll Awhile at Jeffield, bred by the late Mrs. D. Field. He won his 4th Challenge Certificate at Crufts in 1983. Owned by Mrs. P. W. Burtenshaw, Pelido Collies, Godalming, Surrey, England.

June Napoli

← **Overleaf:**

Ch. Glen Hill Campus Cutie finished at the Collie Club of Georgia Specialty, April 1984, with Best of Winners, then Best of Opposite Sex over specials; also winner of the Hunter Memorial Trophy at the Collie Club of America Specialty 1983, awarded for Best American-bred. Owned by Patricia Starkweather and Ron Folse.

Overleaf: →

1. Can. Ch. Tricounty Rambling Rose, by Am. and Can. Ch. Twin Creek's Damn Yankee ex Can. Ch. Lamour's Midnight Fantasy, pictured finishing her title at St. Catherine's 1984. Owned by Brian and Hazel Hampson, Tricounty Kennels, Jarvis, Ontario.

2. Ch. Lisara's Morning After, by Ch. Sunkist Midnight Flyer ex Ch. Lisara's After Knight Delight, was born 1981. Bred and owned by Lawrence and Carmen Leonard, Rockwell, Texas.

3. Can. Ch. Honeybun's Smoke Screen, by Honeybun's Super Charge ex Ch. Honeybun's Blue Nun O'Charisma, bred by Shirley Dowski, has U.S. points, and at a big Specialty in Canada was Best of Opposite Sex. Owned by Wendy and Wally Ace, South Mountain, Ontario, Canada.

4. Aust. Ch. Einar Chandelier Blue, by Aust. Ch. Fairloch Performer ex Aust. Ch. Milbalind Blue Mandy, famous winner owned by Einar Kennels, Kaleen, Australia.

5. Ch. Scotchskye's Lotta Pizzaz at age six months is by Ch. Ryerlea's Evening Breeze ex Scotchskye's Gold Sheena. Bred and owned by Sandra Campbell, Nova Scotia, Canada.

6. Silcrest Xtriordinaire, C.D., by Ch. Wickmere Silver Bullet ex Silcrest Sylver Myst, owned by Marlene R. Nicholson, Hendersonville, Tennessee. Pictured taking Reserve Winners from the puppy class.

163

← **Overleaf:**

1. El Solo Karob The Bare Facts, Smooth Collie by Glenecho Royal Dynasty ex Sumerhill's Heir Express, a smashing young bitch bred by the Norstroms who co-own her with Mr. and Mrs. Robert Frost.

2. Silver Smoke of Clendon Brook at nine months of age. This son of Ch. Elegy Brigadoon ex Ch. Elegy Aida was bred by Linda Goldfarb, Elegy Kennels. Owned by Christine Stewart, Glens Falls, New York.

3. Am. and Can. Ch. Mountainblue's Silver Magician is by Can. Ch. Nationview's Jewell's Pirate ex Can. Ch. Mountainblue's Touch of Magic. Owned by Wendy and Wally Ace, South Mountain, Ontario, Canada.

4. Ch. Highfields Whispering Hope, by Ch. Wickmere Silver Bullet ex Ch. Highfields Debutante, finished title with three majors as a puppy and was dam of Best Puppy in Show at the 1982 Collie Club of America Speciality. She is one of four champions in her litter. Bred by Nancy McDonald and Mary Fields, Manassas, Virginia.

5. Ch. Lisara's Seaview Nightingdale, noted Smooth Collie by Ch. The Blue Baron of Arrowhill ex Ch. Seaview's Lark of Kasan, born in 1975 is the dam of 13 champions in four litters. Bred by Florence Lippman. Owned by Lawrence and Carmen Leonard, Rockwall, Texas.

6. The Smooth Collie Ch. Sumerhill Special Delivery, noted Speciality and Group placement winner, owned by El Solo Kennels, Richard and Marjorie Norstrom, Honolulu, Hawaii.

1. Eng. Ch. Ugony's FairDinkum and Eng. Ch. Ugony's That's My Shiela are owned by Miss D. M. Young, Lopen, Somerset, England. These littermates are by Eng. Ch. Duntiblae Dingo ex Ugony's Harvest Festival. Shiela, on the *right,* is the 1984 Top Winning Collie Bitch in England, with eight Challenge Certificates.

2. Ch. Wickmere Silver Bullet winning the Stud Dog Class at the 1982 Collie Club of America Specialty with his two sons, Ch. Barksdale Best Dressed (tri-color) and Ch. Stoneybrook Silver Saint C.D. (blue merle). Bullet was owned by the Rooses of Fairfax, Virginia. Best Dressed is owned by the Reddings of Pennsylvania. Silver Saint is owned by Kathy Moll and Mrs. R. Fairbanks of North Carolina.

1▲

2▼

← **Overleaf:**

1. Ch. Windarla's World Seeker, *left,* and Can. Ch. Kairlake Moonlight Sonata, the latter winning her first U.S. point under Herman Fellton, Piedmont K.C., July 1983. Sonata is by Can. Ch. Shamont Silver Dollar (Ch. Ravette's The Silver Meteor son) ex Can. Ch. Lickcreek's Classic Rhythm. Both owned by Marlene and Ewing Nicholson. Sonata bred by Kas Majcher and Irene Majcher. Was handled to Canadian title by 17-year old Laurie Majcher.

2. Littermates completing their championships on the same occasion. On the *right,* Ch. Scotchskye's Blond on Blond, sable bitch winning Best of Breed. On the *left,* Ch. Scotchskye's Scotch and Gentle, tri-dog, winning Best of Opposite Sex. Product of a father-to-daughter breeding, by Ch. Ryerlea's Evening Breeze ex Scotchskye's Gold Sheena. Bred by Sandra Campbell, co-owner with Hugh Campbell, Scotchskye Kennels, Nova Scotia, Canada.

1. Ch. Azalea Hill's Strike Force, a young male of most beautiful expression, here at age nine months, taking Winners Dog for two points at Macon Kennel Club. Owned by Mrs. Richmond Fairbanks, Greenville, South Carolina.

2. Ch. Alliance's Amiable Amy is by Henderson's Dandy Man (full brother to World Seeker) from Le Creek's Gold Alliance (daughter of Champion Tamarack Eclipse, granddaughter of Ch. Hanover's I Am Legend). Owned by Ewing and Marlene Nicholson and bred by Marlene Nicholson and S. Shalibo. This recently crowned niece of World Seeker is expected to be his future bride.

3. Ch. Barksdale Best Dressed taking Winners Dog at the Collie Club of Maryland in 1982. Judge was Mr. Yoshio Mori of Japan. Shelly Roos handled. Best Dressed is from a litter of four champions sired by Ch. Wickmere Silver Bullet ex Ch. Highefields Debutante. Bred by Nancy McDonald and Mary Fields. Nancy McDonald, owner, Manassas, Virginia.

4. Belle's Alliance With Venus, by Ch. Tamarack Eclipse (Ch. Tamarack Asterisk son) ex Lakshmi's Magic, C.D. (Ch. Hanover's I Am Legend daughter), was Winners Bitch and Best of Opposite Sex at Tuscaloosa in 1981. Handled by George E. Schlinker for Marlene and Ewing Nicholson, Hendersonville, Tennessee.

← **Overleaf:**

1. Deep River's Time Lord taking a major his first time out at six months of age. Bred by Kathy V. Moll, co-owner with Mrs. Richmond Fairbanks and Christine Warren.

2. Future Ch. White Cloud's Bewitch'n Harvest at six months of age. This marvelously promising puppy, by Honey Hill Harvester ex The White Cloud's Spring Harvest, was bred by Linda De EvLis, co-owner with Carmen Leonard.

3. Ch. Elegy Aida, by Ch. Berridale Macdega Mediator ex Kinmont Elegy, bred by Kinmont Kennels. Owned by Linda Goldfarb, Elegy Collies, Ballston Spa, New York.

4. Ch. Braetana Let It Shine, by Ch. Glenecho Set The Style ex Ch. Braetana Verra Blue, bred in Montana by Jane Akers. Owned in Hawaii by Richard and Marjorie Norstrom.

1. Ch. Azalea Hill's Windhover, C.D. was the first champion owned by Kathy V. Moll, and was co-owned by Mrs. Richmond Fairbanks. Pictured winning Best of Variety his first time out as a special at Lumberton in 1980.

2. Ch. Impromptu The Silver Bullet, by Impromptu The Brown Bomber ex Afterhours Ingenue, finished title in 1980. Owner-bred by Barbara Schwartz.

3. Ch. Glen Hill Flashback by Glen Hill Dorian Gray ex Ch. Briarhill Midnight High, with Patricia Starkweather in 1982. Bred by Patricia Starkweather and Judy Klosterman, owned by Mr. and Mrs. D. F. Starkweather.

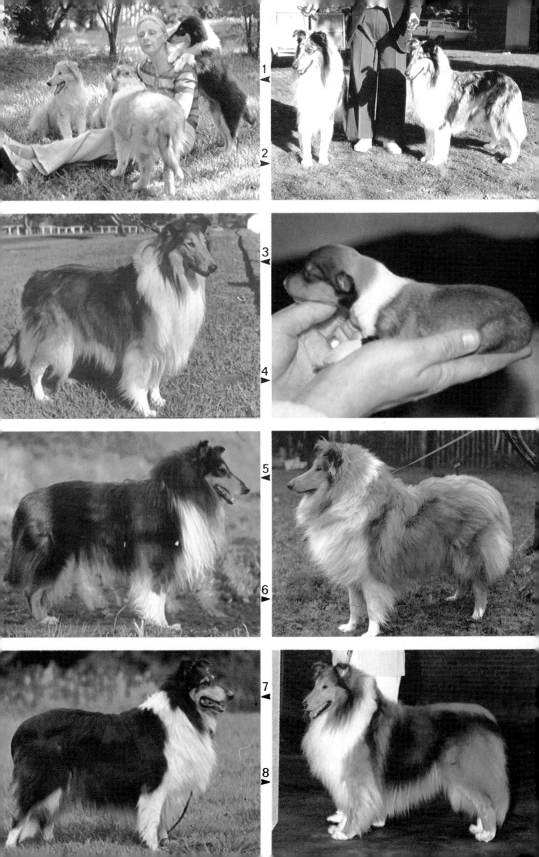

← **Overleaf:**

1. "Fun in the garden," from Australia, a collection of Hylinden puppies.

2. *Left,* Aust. Ch. Einar Blue Dynasty, by Aust. Ch. Fairloch Performer ex Aust. Ch. Milbalind Blue Mandy, with Aust. Ch. Einar Chandelier Blue, *right.* Owned by Einar Kennels, Bill and Joan Ranie, Kaleen, A.C.T., Australia.

3. Aust. Ch. Hylinden Sapper owned by Mrs. J. Bruce, Mittagong, New South Wales, Australia.

4. Future Champion Tricounty's Rambling Rose at exactly one day old. Owned by Brian and Hazel Hampson, Tricounty Kennels, Jarvis, Ontario, Canada.

5. Ch. Ryerlea's Evening Breeze at age ten years. This foundation male at Canada's famed Scotchskye Kennels is owned by Sandra and Hugh Campbell. Evening Breeze was bred by Janet Ryerson.

6. Pelido Double Fantasy, by Ch. Arranbrook Mr. Chips of Aberhill ex Pelido French Knickers, owned and bred by Mr. and Mrs. P. W. Burtenshaw, Pelido Kennels, Godalming, Surrey, England. Double Fantasy is the winner of Junior Warrant, one Challenge Certificate and one Reserve Challenge Certificate.

7. Crown Royal Midnight Mood at ten years of age in 1974; the foundation bitch for Impromptu' Collies owned by Barbara Schwartz, Hollis, New Hampshire.

8. Ch. Azalea Hill's Top Man, the Nation's No. 1 Collie for 1980 and Best in Specialty Show at the Collie Club of America National that year, is pictured here taking a Working Group placement at Greenville Kennel Club in 1979. Judge was Tom Gately. George Schlinker handled for breeder, Mrs. Richmond Fairbanks, and co-owners Mr. and Mrs. T. C. Livingston.

Overleaf: →

1. Deep River's Silver Standard is by Ch. Stoneybrook Silver Saint, C.D. ex Lizdon's Merry Frolicker. This pointed son of Silver Saint is pictured here winning Best in Match at an all-breed event. Owned by Kathy V. Moll.

2. Richard Norstrom with Ch. Akirene's Counter Force and a promising puppy by this famous dog at El Solo Kennels, Honolulu, Hawaii.

3. Ch. Piney Branch Octobersong was bred and is owned by Pat Loos of Piney Branch Collies in Virginia. This son of Ch. Shamont Stormalong ex Shamont Peaches 'N Cream is a Group winner with several Specialty Shows as well to his credit.

4. Ch. Mariner Castles In The Air, born 1979, by Ch. Shamont Stormalong ex Ch. Shamont Sand Castles, C.D., is a homebred Collie owned by Margaret and James C. Vohr. She finished her championship with two Specialty majors, now a multiple Group winner.

5. Cownbred Trisatin at Laureats owned by Mrs. Y. Gillibrand, Gorton, Manchester, England.

6. These top show puppies by Ch. Glen Hill Show Boy are owned by Patricia Starkweather, Glen Hill Kennels, Middleburg, Florida.

1

2

3

4

5

6

← **Overleaf:**

1. Limelight at Laureats owned by Mrs. Y. Gillibrand, Gorton, Manchester, England.

2. The tri-color is La Di Da at Laureats; the sable and white, Limelight at Laureats. Both Smooth Collies are owned by Mrs. Y. Gillibrand, Gorton, Manchester, England.

3. The promising puppy Pelido Midnight Scandal, by Ch. Jeffield Esquire ex Pelido Polar Eclipse, owned by Mr. G. Catalano of Rome, Italy. Bred by Mr. and Mrs. P. W. Burtenshaw, Pelido, Godalming, Surrey, England.

4. Aust. Ch. Einar Blue Dynasty, by Fairloch Flashback ex Aust. Ch. Milbalind Blue Mandy, owned by Einar Collies, Bill and Joan Ranie, Kaleen, A.C.T., Australia.

5. Einar Blue Tradition, by Fairloch Performer ex Aust. Ch. Milbalind Blue Mandy, owned by Einar Kennels of Bill and Joan Ranie, Kaleen, A.C.T., Australia.

6. Foxearth Lord Fountleroy at Laureates, by Eng. Ch. Astrellita The Silversmith ex Foxearth Frappant, owned by Mrs. Y. Gillibrand, Gorton, Manchester, England.

Overleaf: →

1. Ch. Shadow Hill's Stormy Sea, C.D.X., tri-color male owned by Mrs. Richmond Fairbanks, Greenville, South Carolina.

2. Ch. Glen Hill Show Boy owned by Margaret Ridgeway and Patricia Starkweather was the winner of the Blue Banner Award for the Top Winning Blue Merle in the United States in 1979, awarded through the Collie Club of America.

1▲

2▼

1▲ 2▼

← **Overleaf:**

1. Pelido Moody Blue, by Ch. Cathanbrae Polar Moon at Pelido ex Pelido Clear Crystal, owned and bred by Mr. and Mrs. P. W. Burtonshaw, Pelido, Godalming, Surrey, England.

2. Int. Ch. Incredibly Blu di Cambriano, famous Challenge Certificate winner, who was adjudged Best in Show by Mrs. H. R. Hunt when she judged in Italy during 1984. This noted British authority was so greatly impressed that she persuaded the owner, Mrs. R. T. Garabelli, to permit her to bring him back with her to England, where she had the pleasure of showing him to an early championship there. Now this magnificent dog is in Sweden becoming a Scandinavian Champion prior to his return home to Italy.

1. Ch. Twin Creeks Mouse That Roared, T.T., by Ch. Twin Creek's True Grit (top producing sire) ex Ch. Twin Creeks Nitty Gritty. Bred by Ben and Joyce Houser, owned by Rebecca L. Tehon, Clay, New York.

2. Ch. Azalea Hill's Sheyne, rough Collie dog, completed his championship by taking Winners Dog under judge Heywood Hoch at Murfreesboro Kennel Club , September 1983. Jon Woodring handled for owner, Mrs. Richmond Fairbanks, Greenville, South Carolina. This is a son of Ch. Azalea's Court Jester ex Azalea Hill's Honey Love, Top Producing Bitch for 1980.

3. Ch. Mariner Barnstormer, born 1979, by Ch. Shamont Stormalong ex Ch. Shamont Sand Castles, C.D. This lovely Group winner is owned by breeders, Margaret and James C. Vohr, Mariner Kennels, Northfield, Massachusetts.

4. Ch. Azalea Hill's Landstar wins Best of Breed over specials, then on to Group 3rd under noted authority Arnold Wolfe at Columbia Kennel Club in 1983. Wade Burns handled for owners, Mrs. Richmond Fairbanks (breeder of this splendid dog) and Mr. and Mrs. T. C. Livingston of San Antonio, Texas.

← **Overleaf:**

1. Ch. Deep River's Crystal Clear with handler Wade Burns taking Best of Winners for a 4-point major on the way to the title. Bred and owned by Kathy V. Moll, Deep River Collies, Pittsboro, North Carolina.

2. Ch. Deep River Even Chances, C.D., taking Best of Winners at Skyline Kennel Club in 1980. This was Kathy Moll's first homebred champion.

3. Alliance's Wonder Whirl, C.D., by Chris Mik's Jim Beam ex Edenrock Diamond In The Ruff, here is going from the puppy class to Best of Breed under judge Vincent Perry at the Savannah Kennel Club 1980. Handled by George Schlinker for owners Marlene Nicholson and Donna M. Barrett.

4. Ch. Glen Hill News Flash is one of the notable Collies owned by Patricia Starkweather, Glen Hill Collies, Middleburg, Florida. Co-owned by June Napoli.

Overleaf: →

Ch. Scotchskye's Scotch and Gentle, age one year, is the product of a father-daughter breeding of Scotchskye's Gold Sheena back to her sire Ch. Ryerlea's Evening Breeze. Bred by Sandra Campbell, co-owner with Hugh Campbell, Scotch-skye Kennels, Kings County, Nova Scotia, Canada.

Chapter 8

Standards of the Breed

The standards of the breed, to which one hears such frequent reference whenever purebred dogs are the subject of discussion, is the word picture of the ideal specimen of that breed of dog. This standard outlines, in specific detail, each and every feature of the individual breed, both physical characteristics and in temperament, minutely describing the dog literally "from whisker to tail," thus creating for the reader a complete mental picture of what is to be considered correct and what is not; the features comprising "breed type"; and the probable temperament and behavior patterns of typical members of the breed.

The standard is the guide for breeders endeavoring to produce quality dogs and for fanciers anxious to learn what is considered beautiful in these dogs; and it is the tool with which judges work in evaluating and reaching their decisions in the show ring.

Prior to the adoption of a breed standard here in the United States, or any revisions to same, endless hours have been spent by dedicated fanciers selected from among the most respected and knowledgeable members of the parent club, in this case the Collie Club of America, for the task of studying the background of the breed, searching out the earliest histories and breed descriptions from the country of origin and along the way throughout the breed's development. This committee's recommendations then come before the entire membership of the parent Specialty Club for further study and discussion, and then they are presented to the American Kennel Club from which approval must be granted prior to a standard or its revisions becoming effective.

From earliest times, most breeds have had as their standards usually informally written descriptions of what owners of the dogs have considered important in developing dogs to fulfill the working requirements and purposes for which these early dogs were intended. As time progressed, more emphasis has been placed on appearance of the dogs and their beauty. Even so, it should never be forgotten that the majority of breeds were originally developed to assist man in some specific manner, and that the basic factors should remain ever present in our efforts to preserve those qualities which were involved with the original creation of the breed.

Ch. Impromptú Instant Carmine finished in 1973. Bred and owned by Barbara Schwartz, Hollis, New Hampshire.

COLLIE CLUB OF AMERICA
OFFICIAL STANDARD FOR THE COLLIE

ROUGH

GENERAL CHARACTER: The Collie is a lithe, strong, responsive, active dog carrying no useless timber, standing naturally straight and firm. The deep, moderately wide chest shows strength, the sloping shoulders and well-bent hocks indicate speed and grace, and the face shows high intelligence. The Collie presents an impressive, proud picture of true balance, each part being in harmonious proportion to every other part and to the whole. Except for the technical description that is essential to this Standard and without which no Standard for the guidance of breeders and judges is adequate, it could be stated simply that no part of the Collie ever seems to be out of proportion to any other part. Timidity, frailness, sullenness, viciousness, lack of animation, cumbersome appearance and lack of overall balance impair the general character.

HEAD: The head properties are of great importance. When considered in proportion to the size of the dog the head is inclined to lightness and never appears massive. A heavy-headed dog lacks the necessary bright, alert, full-of-sense look that contributes so greatly to expression. Both in front and profile view the head bears a general resemblance to a well blunted lean wedge, being smooth and clean in outline and nicely balanced in proportion. On the sides it tapers gradually and smoothly from the ears to the end of the black nose without being flared out in backskull ("cheeky") or pinched in muzzle ("snipy"). In profile view the top of the backskull and the top of the muzzle lie in two approximately parallel, straight planes of equal length, divided by a very slight but perceptible stop or break.

A mid point between the inside corners of the eyes (which is the center of a correctly placed stop) is the center of balance in length of head.

The end of the smooth, well rounded muzzle is blunt but not square. The under-jaw is strong, clean-cut, and the depth of skull from the brow to the under part of the jaw is not excessive.

The teeth are of good size meeting in a scissors bite. *Overshot or undershot jaws are undesirable, the latter being more severely penalized.*

There is a very slight prominence of the eyebrows. The back-skull is flat, without receding either laterally or backward and the occipital bone is not highly peaked. The proper width of backskull necessarily depends upon the combined length of skull and muzzle and the width of the backskull is less than its length. Thus the correct width varies with the individual and is dependent upon the extent to which it is supported by length of muzzle.

Because of the importance of the head characteristics, *prominent head faults are very severely penalized.*

EYES: Because of the combination of the flat skull, the arched eyebrows, the slight stop and the rounded muzzle, the foreface must be chiseled to form a receptacle for the eyes and they are necessarily placed obliquely to give them the required forward outlook. Except for the blue merles, they are required to be matched in color. They are almond shaped, of medium size, and never properly appear to be large or prominent. The color is dark and the eye does not show a yellow ring or a sufficiently prominent haw to affect the dog's expression. The eyes have a clear, bright appearance, expressing intelligent inquisitiveness, particularly when the ears are drawn up and the dog is on the alert. In blue merles, dark brown eyes are preferable, but either or both eyes may be merle or china in color without specific penalty. A large, round, full eye seriously detracts from the desired "sweet" expression. *Eye faults are heavily penalized.*

EARS: The ears are in proportion to the size of the head and, if they are carried properly and unquestionably "break" naturally, are seldom too small. Large ears usually cannot be lifted correctly off the head, and even if lifted they will be out of proportion to the size of the head. When in repose, the ears are folded lengthwise and thrown back into the frill. On the alert they are drawn well up on the backskull and are carried about three-quarters erect, with about one-fourth of the ear tipping or "breaking" forward. *A dog with prick ears or low ears cannot show true expression and is penalized accordingly.*

NECK: The neck is firm, clean, muscular, sinewy and heavily frilled. It is fairly long, carried upright with a slight arch at the nape and imparts a proud, upstanding appearance showing off the frill.

BODY: The body is firm, hard and muscular, a trifle long in proportion to the height. The ribs are well-rounded behind the

well- sloped shoulders and the chest is deep, extending to the elbows. The back is strong and level, supported by powerful hips and thighs, and the croup is sloped to give a well-rounded finish. The loin is powerful and slightly arched. Noticeably fat dogs, or dogs in poor flesh or with skin disease or with no undercoat are out of condition and are moderately penalized accordingly.

LEGS: The forelegs are straight and muscular, with a fair amount of bone considering the size of the dog. A cumbersome appearance is undesirable. Both narrow and wide placement are penalized. The forearm is moderately fleshy and the pasterns are flexible but without weakness. The hind legs are less fleshy, muscular at the thighs, very sinewy, and the hocks and stifles are well bent. *A cowhocked dog or a dog with straight stifles is penalized.* The comparatively small feet are approximately oval in shape. The soles are well-padded and tough, and the toes are well arched and close together. When the Collie is not in motion the legs and feet are judged by allowing the dog to come to a natural stop in a standing position so that both the forelegs and the hind legs are placed well apart, with the feet extending straight forward. Excessive "posing" is undesirable.

GAIT: Gait is sound. When the dog is moved at a slow trot toward an observer its straight front legs track comparatively close together at the ground. The front legs are not out at the elbows, do not "cross over" nor does the dog move with a choppy, pacing or rolling gait. When viewed from the rear the hind legs are straight, tracking comparatively close together at the ground. At a moderate trot the hindlegs are powerful and propelling. Viewed from the side, the reasonably long "reaching" stride is smooth and even, keeping the back line firm and level.

As the speed of the gait is increased the Collie single tracks, bringing the front legs inward in a straight line from the shoulder toward the center line of the body and the hind legs inward in a straight line from the hip toward the center line of the body. The gait suggests effortless speed combined with the dog's herding heritage, requiring it to be capable of changing its direction of travel almost instantaneously.

TAIL: The tail is moderately long, the bone reaching to the hock joint or below. It is carried low when the dog is quiet, the end having an upward twist or "swirl." When gaited or when the dog is excited it is carried gaily but not over the back.

COAT: The well-fitting, proper-textured coat is the crowning glory of the rough variety of Collie. It is abundant except on the head and legs. The outer coat is straight and harsh to the touch. *A soft, open outer coat or a curly outer coat, regardless of quantity, is penalized.* The undercoat, however, is soft, furry, and so close together that is is difficult to see the skin when the hair is parted. The coat is very abundant on the mane and frill. The face or mask is smooth. The forelegs are smooth and well feathered to the back of the pasterns. The hind legs are smooth below the hock joints. Any feathering below the hocks is removed for the show ring. The hair on the tail is very profuse and on the hips it is long and bushy. The texture, quantity, and the extent to which the coat "fits the dog" are important points.

COLOR: The four recognized colors are "Sable and White," "Tri- Color," "Blue Merle," and "White." There is no preference among them. The "Sable and White" is predominantly sable (a fawn sable color of varying shades from light gold to dark mahogany) with white markings usually on the chest, neck, legs, feet, and the tip of the tail. A blaze may appear on the foreface or backskull or both. The "Tri- Color" is predominantly black, carrying white markings as in a "Sable and White" and has tan shadings on and about the head and legs. The "Blue Merle" is a mottled or "marbled" color predominantly blue- gray and black with white markings as in the "Sable and White" and usually has tan shadings as in the "Tri-Color." The "White" is predominantly white, preferably with sable, tri-color or blue merle markings.

SIZE: Dogs are from 24 to 26 inches at the shoulder and weigh from 60 to 75 pounds. Bitches are from 22 to 24 inches at the shoulder, weighing from 60 to 65 pounds. *An undersize or an oversize Collie is penalized according to the extent to which the dog appears to be undersize or oversize.*

EXPRESSION: Expression is one of the most important points in considering the relative value of Collies. "Expression," like the term "character," is difficult to define in words. It is not a fixed point as in color, weight or height and it is something the uninitiated can properly understand only by optical illustration. In general, however, it may be said to be the combined product of the shape and balance of the skull and muzzle, the placement, size, shape, and color of the eye, and the position, size, and carriage of the ears. An expression that shows sullenness or which is suggestive of any other breed is entirely foreign. The Collie cannot be judged properly until its expression has been carefully evaluated.

SMOOTH

The Smooth Variety of Collie is judged by the same Standard as the Rough Variety, except that the references to the quantity and the distribution of the coat are not applicable to the Smooth Collie which has a short, hard, dense, flat coat of good texture with an abundance of undercoat.

KENNEL CLUB (ENGLISH) VARIATION TO STANDARD

The Kennel Club considers the rough-coated and smooth-coated varieties of Collies as two separate breeds.

COLOR: three only, sable, tri-color, and blue merles.

WEIGHT: dogs 45 to 65 pounds and bitches 40 to 55 pounds.

Left, Pelido Polar Eclipse. *Right,* Pelido Hot Chocolate. Four-month-old puppies bred by Mr. and Mrs. P. W. Burtonshaw, Pelido Collies, England. Sire of puppies, Ch. Cathambrae Polar Moon at Pelido; dam, Pelido Eclipse over Jeffield.

Chapter 9

Versatility of the Collie

Probably one of the reasons Collies have been so highly admired throughout the years is the versatility which enables them to fit so perfectly into many roles and many situations. Here, indeed, is a dog who can be "all things to all people." Superbly intelligent, capable, strong, and beautiful, practically brimming over with *joie de vivre*, the Collie is a very special member of the canine community.

Being instinctively a working dog, the Collie makes a useful, well appreciated member of a farming family. He is fearless in the face of danger, particularly should that danger be directed towards a member of his family, and seems to know almost instinctively when a perilous situation exists as can be proven by the many life-saving hero dogs in the history of this breed. He has served, with regularity, as the eyes for a blind person and as ears for a deaf person, earning esteem as he does so. He has done his share in times of war. He has a good police record as a narcotics dog who has sniffed out marijuana with brilliant results, to mention a few of his more heroic accomplishments.

As a member of your family where his chief "job" is that of being your friend and companion, no dog could more ideally fill the bill. Kind and gentle, he is a perfect dog for children, with whom he obviously possesses a special rapport, enjoying their attention and games whether they be toddlers or teen-agers. He seems to have an almost uncanny sense of responsibility where youngsters

Lynn Goldfarb is a talented artist, and she shares with us some of the portraits she has done of her Elegy Collies. This one, "Waiting For Santa" is a favorite with the author.

are concerned, and has a long record of occasions when his loyalty and intelligence have "saved the day" in preventing harm to them.

As a Collie owner, you will find yourself with a very pleasant dog to have around. Quiet, dignified, and reserved upon occasion, he also can be brimming over with animation and fun. If you are in the mood for outdoor activity, he will join you with glee. If you are more inclined to read or watch television in your leisure time, he will share that, too, with his head on your knee or lying alongside your chair, patiently snoozing.

If you are choosing a breed of dog with whom to compete in any field of dog show activity, here again the Collie is an ideal choice. His intelligence and delight in pleasing you have made him an excellent dog in obedience competition all along the line. He has helped many a junior handler to success. And he is an impressive dog in the show ring, so very beautiful and elegant, that to exhibit a Collie fills one with pride.

The Collie is quite at home in your living room, being not a destructive dog, and if properly cared for, his coat is little problem, doing most of its shedding all at one time, thus getting it over within a short period. A good bath when the shedding starts will bring the old coat out quickly, and frequent brushing will keep the loose hair off the furniture.

If you live in the city and feel that no other dog will please you except a Collie, by all means have one—that is, of course, if you are planning to really spend a bit of time with the dog, and are willing to provide a walking excursion a couple of times daily to keep him in trim. While I would not especially recommend a dog of this size and with so much coat becoming an apartment dweller, it can certainly be worked out satisfactorily. But the Collie is in his greatest element living in the country where, given the slightest opportunity, his instinct to "ply his trade" seems to take over.

Actually I am sure there is little I can add to all that has been written in the past regarding the fabulous talents of a Collie. Albert Payson Terhune planted the seed in all our minds with *Lad: A Dog* and stories of the other Sunnybank Collies, for who among us did not grow up reading them and wishing for a dog just like the ones at "Sunnybank"? Then along came Eric Knight with *Lassie Come Home* which, through book, motion pictures and television has reached literally millions of people. With two authors such as these going for it, the Collie breed has had its merits accurately and widely called to the attention of animal lovers around the world, and I am certain that the number of people who own Collies because of their original impression of them from these writings add up to a fantastic total. If ever a dog lives up to its press coverage, it is the Collie. The acclaim and popularity could not possibly have happened to a better breed.

Head study of the excellent Ch. Travler's Flim Flam Man, by Ch. Gin Geor Jack of Tamarack ex River'Odes Bonnie Gay Lady, bred and owned by   S. W. Tehon, Clay, New York. He was Winners Dog at the Presque Isle Collie Club Specialty.

Chapter 10

The Purchase of Your Collie

Careful consideration should be given to what breed of dog you wish to own prior to your purchase of one. If several breeds are attractive to you, and you are undecided as to which you prefer, learn all you can about the characteristics of each before making your decision. As you do so, you are thus preparing yourself to make an intelligent choice; and this is very important when buying a dog who will be, with reasonable luck, a member of your household for at least a dozen years or more. Obviously since you are reading this book, you have decided on the breed—so now all that remains is to make a good choice.

It is never wise to just rush out and buy the first cute puppy who catches your eye. Whether you wish a dog to show, one with whom to compete in obedience, or one as a family dog purely for his (or her) companionship, the more time and thought you invest as you plan the purchase, the more likely you are to meet with complete satisfaction. The background and early care behind your pet will reflect in the dog's future health and temperament. Even if you are planning the purchase purely as a pet, with no thoughts of showing or breeding in the dog's or puppy's future, it is essential that if the dog is to enjoy a trouble-free future you assure yourself of a healthy, properly raised puppy or adult from sturdy, well-bred stock.

Throughout the pages of this book you will find the names and locations of many well-known and well-established kennels in various areas. Another source of information is the American Kennel Club (51 Madison Avenue, New York, New York 10010) from whom you can obtain a list of recognized breeders in the vicinity of your home. If you plan to have your dog campaigned by a professional handler, by all means let the handler help you locate and select a good dog. Through their numerous clients, handlers have access to a variety of interesting show prospects; and the usual arrangement is that the handler re-sells the dog to you for what his cost has been, with the agreement that the dog be campaigned for you by him throughout the dog's career. It is most strongly recommended that prospective purchasers follow these suggestions, as you thus will be better able to locate and select a satisfactory puppy or dog.

Your first step in searching for your puppy is to make appointments at kennels specializing in the chosen breed, where you can visit and inspect the dogs, both those available for sale and the kennel's basic breeding stock. You are looking for an active, sturdy puppy with bright eyes and intelligent expression and who is friendly and alert; avoid puppies who are hyperactive, dull, or listless. The coat should be clean and thick, with no sign of parasites. The premises on which he was raised should look (and smell) clean and be tidy, making it obvious that the puppies and their surroundings are in capable hands. Should the kennels featuring the breed you intend owning be sparse in your area or not have what you consider attractive, do not hesitate to contact others at a distance and purchase from them if they seem better able to supply a puppy or dog who will please you *so long as it is a recognized breeding kennel of that breed.* Shipping dogs is a regular practice nowadays, with comparatively few problems when one considers the number of dogs shipped each year. A reputable, well-known breeder wants the customer to be satisfied; thus he will represent the puppy fairly. Should you not be pleased with the puppy upon arrival, a breeder such as described will almost certainly permit its return. A conscientious breeder takes real interest and concern in the welfare of the dogs he or she causes to be brought into the world. Such a breeder also is proud of a reputation for integrity. Thus on two counts, for the sake of the dog's future and the breeder's reputation, to such a person a *satisfied* customer takes precedence over a sale at any cost.

If your puppy is to be a pet or "family dog," the earlier the age at which it joins your household the better. Puppies are weaned and ready to start out on their own, under the care of a sensible new owner, at about six weeks old; and if you take a young one, it is often easier to train it to the routine of your household and to your requirements of it than is the case with an older dog which, even though still a puppy technically, may have already started habits you will find difficult to change. The younger puppy is usually less costly, too, as it stands to reason the breeder will not have as much expense invested in it. Obviously, a puppy that has been raised to five or six months old represents more in care and cash expenditure on the breeder's part than one sold earlier and therefore should be and generally is priced accordingly.

There is an enormous amount of truth in the statement that "bargain" puppies seldom turn out to be that. A "cheap" puppy, cheaply raised purely for sale and profit, can and often does lead to great heartbreak including problems and veterinarian's bills which can add up to many times the initial cost of a properly reared dog. On the other hand, just because a puppy is expensive does not assure one that is healthy and well reared. There have been numerous cases where unscrupulous dealers have sold for several hundred dollars puppies that were sickly, in poor condition, and such poor specimens that the breed of which they were supposedly members was barely recognizable. So one cannot always judge a puppy by price alone. Common sense must guide a prospective purchaser, plus the selection of a *reliable*, well-recommended dealer whom you know to have well satisfied customers or, best of all, a specialized breeder. You will probably find the fairest pricing at the kennel of a breeder. Such a person, experienced with the breed in general and with his or her own stock in particular, through extensive association with these dogs has watched enough of them mature to have obviously learned to assess quite accurately each puppy's potential—something impossible where such background is non-existent.

One more word on the subject of pets. Bitches make a fine choice for this purpose as they are usually quieter and more gentle than the males, easier to house train, more affectionate, and less inclined to roam. If you do select a bitch and have no intention of breeding or showing her, by all means have her spayed, for your sake and for hers. The advantages to the owner of a spayed bitch include avoiding the nuisance of "in season" periods which normally occur twice yearly, with the accompanying eager canine swains haunting your premises in an effort to get close to your female, plus the unavoidable messiness and spotting of furniture and rugs at this time, which can be annoying if she is a household companion in the habit of sharing your sofa or bed. As for the spayed bitch, she benefits as she grows older because this simple operation almost entirely eliminates the possibility of breast cancer ever occurring. It is recommended that all bitches eventually be spayed—even those used for show or breeding when their careers have ended—in order that they may enjoy a happier, healthier old age. Please take note, however, that a bitch who has been spayed (or an altered dog) *cannot be shown at American Kennel Club dog shows once this operation has been performed.* Be certain that you are *not* interested in showing her before taking this step.

Also, in selecting a pet, never underestimate the advantages of an older dog, perhaps a retired show dog or a bitch no longer needed for breeding, who may be available quite reasonably priced by a breeder anxious to place such a dog in a loving home. These dogs are settled and can be a delight to own, as they make wonderful companions, especially in a household of adults where raising a puppy can sometimes be a trial.

Everything that has been said about careful selection of your pet puppy and its place of purchase applies, but with many further considerations, when you plan to buy a show dog or foundation stock for a future breeding program. Now is the time for an in-depth study of the breed, starting with every word and every illustration in this book and all others you can find written on the subject. The Standard of the breed now has become your guide, and you must learn not only the words but also how to interpret them and how they are applicable in actual dogs before you are ready to make an intelligent selection of a show dog.

If you are thinking in terms of a dog to show, obviously you must have learned about dog shows and must be in the habit of attending them. This is fine, but now your activity in this direction should be increased, with your attending every single dog show within a reasonable distance from your home. Much can be learned about a breed at ringside at these events. Talk with the breeders who are exhibiting. Study the dogs they are showing.

The handsome dog, Evana Gambler's Touch, handled by Miss Leslie Canavan to win the Collie Club of Long Island 1962 Specialty for Mrs. Evelyn L. Nute.

Watch the judging with concentration, noting each decision made, and attempt to follow the reasoning by which the judge has reached it. Note carefully the attributes of the dogs who win and, for your later use, the manner in which each is presented. Close your ears to the ringside know-it-alls, usually novice owners of only a dog or two and very new to the Fancy, who have only derogatory remarks to make about all that is taking place unless they happen to win. This is the type of exhibitor who "comes and goes" through the Fancy and whose interest is usually of very short duration owing to lack of knowledge and dissatisfaction caused by the failure to recognize the need to learn. You, as a fancier it is hoped will last and enjoy our sport over many future years, should develop independent thinking at this stage; you should learn to draw your own conclusions about the merits, or lack of them, seen before you in the ring and, thus, sharpen your own judgement in preparation for choosing wisely and well.

Note carefully which breeders campaign winning dogs, not just an occasional isolated good one but consistent, homebred winners. It is from one of these people that you should select your own future "star."

If you are located in an area where dog shows take place only occasionally or where there are long travel distances involved, you will need to find another testing ground for your ability to select a worthy show dog. Possibly, there are some representative kennels raising this breed within a reasonable distance. If so, by all means ask permission of the owners to visit the kennels and do so when permission is granted. You may not necessarily buy then and there, as they may not have available what you are seeking that very day, but you will be able to see the type of dog being raised there and to discuss the dogs with the breeder. Every time you do this, you add to your knowledge. Should one of these kennels have dogs which especially appeal to you, perhaps you could reserve a show-prospect puppy from a coming litter. This is frequently done, and it is often worth waiting for a puppy, unless you have seen a dog with which you truly are greatly impressed and which is immediately available.

The purchase of a puppy has already been discussed. Obviously this same approach applies in a far greater degree when the purchase involved is a future show dog. The only place at which to purchase a show prospect is from a breeder who raises show-type stock; otherwise, you are almost certainly doomed to disappointment as the puppy matures. Show and breeding kennels obviously cannot keep all of their fine young stock. An active breeder-exhibitor is, therefore, happy to place promising youngsters in the hands of people also interested in showing and winning with them, doing so at a fair price according to the quality and prospects of the dog involved. Here again, if no kennel in your immediate area has what you are seeking, do not hesitate to contact top breeders in other areas and to buy at long distance. Ask for pictures, pedigrees, and a complete description. Heed the breeder's

Ch. Brandwyne No Foolin' was Winners Dog at Westminster in 1956, then returned in '57 to take Best of Breed there and third in the Working Group. Owned by Sophie Peckelis, Great Neck, New York.

advice and recommendations, after truthfully telling exactly what your expectations are for the dog you purchase. Do you want something with which to win just a few ribbons now and then? Do you want a dog who can complete his championship? Are you thinking of the real "big time" (*i.e.*, seriously campaigning with Best of Breed, Group wins, and possibly even Best in Show as your eventual goal)? Consider it all carefully in advance; then honestly discuss your plans with the breeder. You will be better satisfied with the results if you do this, as the breeder is then in the best position to help you choose the dog who is most likely to come through for you. A breeder selling a show dog is just as anxious as the buyer for the dog to succeed, and the breeder will represent the dog to you with truth and honesty. Also, this type of breeder does not lose interest the moment the sale has been made but when necessary will be right there ready to assist you with beneficial advice and suggestions based on years of experience.

As you make inquiries of at least several kennels, keep in mind that show-prospect puppies are less expensive than mature show dogs, the latter often costing close to four figures, and sometimes more. The reason for this is that, with a puppy, there is always an element of chance, the possibility of its developing unexpected faults as it matures or failing to develop the excellence and quality that earlier had seemed probable. There definitely is a risk factor in buying a show- prospect puppy. Sometimes all goes well, but occasionally the swan becomes an ugly duckling. Reflect on this as you consider available puppies and young adults. It just might be a good idea to go with a more mature, though more costly, dog if one you like is available.

When you buy a mature show dog, "what you see is what you get," and it is not likely to change beyond coat and condition which are dependent on your care. Also advantageous for a novice owner is the fact that a mature dog of show quality almost certainly will have received show-ring training and probably match-show experience, which will make your earliest handling ventures far easier.

Frequently it is possible to purchase a beautiful dog who has completed championship but who, owing to similarity in blood-lines, is not needed for the breeder's future program. Here you have the opportunity of owning a champion, usually in the two-to-five-year-old range, which you can enjoy campaigning as a special (for Best of Breed competition) and which will be a settled, handsome dog for you and your family to enjoy with pride.

If you are planning foundation for a future kennel, concentrate on acquiring one or two really superior bitches. These need not necessarily be top show-quality, but they should represent your breed's finest producing bloodlines from a strain noted for producing quality, generation after generation. A proven matron who is already the dam of show-type puppies is, of course, the ideal selection; but these are usually difficult to obtain, no one being anxious to part with so valuable an asset. You just might strike it lucky, though, in which case you are off to a flying start. If you cannot find such a matron available, select a young bitch of finest background from top-producing lines who is herself of decent type, free of obvious faults, and of good quality.

212

Great attention should be paid to the pedigree of the bitch from whom you intend to breed. If not already known to you, try to see the sire and dam. It is generally agreed that someone starting with a breed should concentrate on a fine collection of topflight bitches and raise a few litters from these before considering keeping one's own stud dog. The practice of buying a stud and then breeding everything you own or acquire to that dog does not always work out well. It is better to take advantage of the many noted sires who are available to be used at stud, who represent all of the leading strains, and in each case to carefully select the one who in type and pedigree seems most compatible to each of your bitches, at least for your first several litters.

To summarize, if you want a "family dog" as a companion, it is best to buy it young and raise it according to the habits of your household. If you are buying a show dog, the more mature it is, the more certain you can be of its future beauty. If you are buying foundation stock for a kennel, then bitches are better, but they must be from the finest *producing* bloodlines.

When you buy a pure-bred dog that you are told is eligible for registration with the American Kennel Club, you are entitled to receive from the seller an application form which will enable you to register your dog. If the seller cannot give you the application form you should demand and receive an identification of your dog consisting of the name of the breed, the registered names and numbers of the sire and dam, the name of the breeder, and your dog's date of birth. If the litter of which your dog is a part is already recorded with the American Kennel Club, then the litter number is sufficient identification.

Do not be misled by promises of papers at some later date. Demand a registration application form or proper identification as described above. If neither is supplied, do not buy the dog. So warns the American Kennel Club, and this is especially important in the purchase of show or breeding stock.

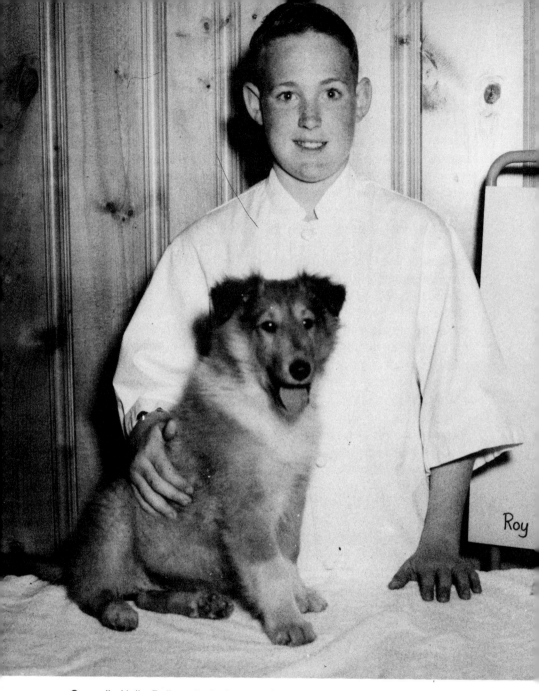

Conrad's Hello Dolly, a typical puppy from this well-known kennel, with Roy Ayers, Jr., some years back. This Collie, in addition to show ring successes, won local, county, and state 4-H competitions in the Veterinary Science project and, another year, in the Dog Care and Training project.

Chapter 11

The Care of Your Collie Puppy

The moment you decide to be the new owner of a puppy is not one second too soon to start planning for the puppy's arrival in your home. Both the new family member and you will find the transition period easier if your home is geared in advance of the arrival.

The first things to be prepared are a bed for the puppy and a place where you can pen him up for rest periods. Every dog should have a crate of its own from the very beginning, so that he will come to know and love it as his special place where he is safe and happy. It is an ideal arrangement, for when you want him to be free, the crate stays open. At other times you can securely latch it and know that the pup is safely out of mischief. If you travel with him, his crate comes along in the car; and, of course, in travelling by plane there is no alternative but to have a carrier for the dog. If you show your dog, you will want him upon occasion to be in a crate a good deal of the day. So from every consideration, a crate is a very sensible and sound investment in your puppy's future safety and happiness and for your own peace of mind.

The crates most desirable are the wooden ones with removable side panels, which are ideal for cold weather (with the panels in place to keep out drafts) and in hot weather (with the panels removed to allow better air circulation). Wire crates are all right in the summer, but they give no protection from cold or drafts. Aluminum crates, due to the manner in which the metal reflects surrounding temperatures, are not recommended. If it is cold, so is the metal of the crate; if it is hot, the crate becomes burning hot.

When you choose the puppy's crate, be certain that it is roomy enough not to become outgrown. The crate should have sufficient height so the dog can stand up in it as a mature dog and sufficient area so that he can stretch out full length when relaxed. When the puppy is young, first give him shredded newspaper as a bed; the papers can be replaced with a mat or turkish towels when the dog is older. Carpet remnants are great for the bottom of the crate, as they are inexpensive and in case of accidents can be quite easily replaced. As the dog matures and is past the chewing age, a pillow or blanket in the crate is an appreciated comfort.

Sharing importance with the crate is a safe area in which the puppy can exercise and play. If you are an apartment dweller, a baby's playpen for a young puppy works out well; for an older puppy use a portable exercise pen which you can use later when travelling with your dog or for dog shows. If you have a yard, an area where he can be outside in safety should be fenced in prior to the dog's arrival at your home. This area does not need to be huge, but it does need to be made safe and secure. If you are in a suburban area where there are close neighbors, stockade fencing works out best as then the neighbors are less aware of the dog and the dog cannot see and bark at everything passing by. If you are out in the country where no problems with neighbors are likely to occur, then regular chain-link fencing is fine. For added precaution in both cases, use a row of concrete blocks or railroad ties inside against the entire bottom of the fence; this precludes or at least considerably lessens the chances of your dog digging his way out.

Be advised that if yours is a single dog, it is very unlikely that it will get sufficient exercise just sitting in the fenced area, which is what most of them do when they are there alone. Two or more dogs will play and move themselves around, but one by itself does little more than make a leisurely tour once around the area to check things over and then lie down. You must include a daily walk or two in your plans if your puppy is to be rugged and well. Exercise is extremely important to a puppy's muscular development and to keep a mature dog fit and trim. So make sure that those exercise periods, or walks, a game of ball, and other such activities, are part of your daily program as a dog owner.

If your fenced area has an outside gate, provide a padlock and key and a strong fastening for it, and use them, so that the gate cannot be opened by others and the dog taken or turned free. The ultimate con-

Devonshire's Rusty Gussy, handsome sable and white owned by Dr. Richard Greathouse and handled by Clint Harris back in the mid-1950's.

venience in this regard is, of course, a door (unused for other purposes) from the house around which the fenced area can be enclosed, so that all you have to do is open the door and out into his area he goes. This arrangement is safest of all, as then you need not be using a gate, and it is easier in bad weather since then you can send the dog out without taking him and becoming soaked yourself at the same time. This is not always possible to manage, but if your house is arranged so that you could do it this way, you would never regret it due to the con-

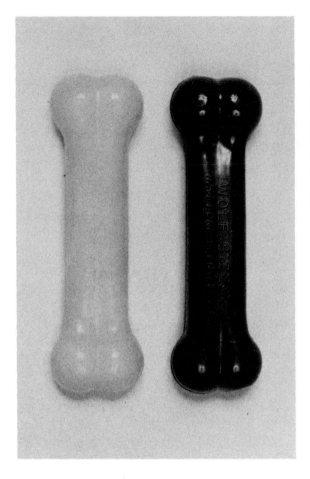

Your Collie will surely enjoy either the meat- or chocolate-flavored Nylabone®. It is regularly available in most pet shops; available in several sizes suitable to different ages and breeds of dogs.

venience and added safety thus provided. Fencing in the entire yard, with gates to be opened and closed whenever a caller, deliveryman, postman, or some other person comes on your property, really is not safe at all because people not used to gates and their importance are frequently careless about closing and latching them *securely*. Many heartbreaking incidents have been brought about by someone carelessly only half closing a gate which the owner had thought to be firmly latched and the dog wandering out. For greatest security a fenced *area* definitely takes precedence over a fenced *yard*.

The puppy will need a collar (one that fits now, not one to be grown into) and lead from the moment you bring him home. Both should be an appropriate weight and type for his size. Also needed are a feeding dish and a water dish, both made preferably of unbreakable material.

Your pet supply shop should have an interesting assortment of these and other accessories from which you can choose. Then you will need grooming tools of the type the breeder recommends and some toys. One of the best toys is a beef bone, either rib, leg, or knuckle (the latter type you can purchase to make soup), cut to an appropriate size for your puppy dog. These are absolutely safe and are great exercise for the teething period, helping to get the baby teeth quickly out of the way with no problems. Equally satisfactory is Nylabone®, a nylon bone that does not chip or splinter and that "frizzles" as the puppy chews, providing healthful gum massage. Rawhide chews are safe, too, *if made in the United States.* There was a problem a few years back, owing to the chemicals with which some foreign rawhide toys had been treated. Also avoid plastics and any sort of rubber toys, *particularly those with squeakers* which the puppy may remove and swallow. If you want a ball for the puppy to use when playing with him, select one of very hard construction made for this purpose and do not leave it alone with him because he may chew off and swallow bits of the rubber. Take the ball with you when the game is over. This also applies to some of those "tug of war" type rubber toys which are fun when used with the two of you for that purpose but again should *not* be left behind for the dog to work on with his teeth. Bits of swallowed rubber, squeakers, and other such foreign articles can wreak great havoc in the intestinal track—do all you can to guard against them.

Too many changes all at once can be difficult for a puppy. For at least the first few days he is with you, keep him on the food and feeding schedule to which he is accustomed. Find out ahead of time from the breeder what he feeds his puppies, how frequently, and at what times of the day. Also find out what, if any, food supplements the breeder has been using and recommends. Then be prepared by getting in a supply of the same food so that you will have it there when you bring the puppy home. Once the puppy is accustomed to his new surroundings, then you can switch the type of food and schedule to fit your convenience, but for the first several days do it as the puppy expects.

Your selection of a veterinarian also should be attended to before the puppy comes home, because you should stop at the vet's office for the puppy to be checked over as soon as you leave the breeder's premises. If the breeder is from your area, ask him for recommendations. Ask your dog-owning friends for their opinions of the local veterinarians, and see what their experiences with those available have been. Choose someone whom several of your friends recommend highly, then contact him about your puppy, perhaps making an appointment to stop in at his office. If the premises are clean, modern, and well equipped, and if you like the veterinarian, make an appointment to bring the puppy in on the day of purchase. Be sure to obtain the puppy's health record from the breeder, including information on such things as shots and wormings that the puppy has had.

JOINING THE FAMILY

Remember that, exciting and happy an occasion as it is for you, the puppy's move from his place of birth to your home can be, for him, a traumatic experience. His mother and littermates will be missed. He quite likely will be awed or frightened by the change of surroundings. The person on whom he depended will be gone. Everything should be planned to make his arrival at your home pleasant—to give him confidence and to help him realize that yours is a pretty nice place to be after all.

Never bring a puppy home on a holiday. There just is too much going on with people and gifts and excitement. If he is in honor of an "occasion," work it out so that his arrival will be a few days earlier or, perhaps even better, a few days later than the "occasion." Then your home will be back to its normal routine and the puppy can enjoy your undivided attention. Try not to bring the puppy home in the evening. Early morning is the ideal time, as then he has the opportunity of getting acquainted and the initial strangeness should wear off before bedtime. You will find it a more peaceful night that way. Allow the puppy to investigate as he likes, under your watchful eye. If you already have a pet in the household, keep a careful watch that the relationship between the two gets off to a friendly start or you may quickly find yourself with a lasting problem. Much of the future attitude of each toward the other will depend on what takes place that first day, so keep your mind on what they are doing and let your other activities slide for the moment. Be careful not to let your older pet become jealous by paying more attention to the puppy than to him, as that will start a bad situation immediately.

If you have a child, here again it is important that the relationship start out well. Before the puppy is brought home, you should have a talk with the youngster about puppies so that it will be clearly understood that puppies are fragile and can easily be injured; therefore, they should not be teased, hurt, mauled, or overly rough-

220

Five of the Conrad Collies relaxing at home. All homebred by Roy L. Ayers, Stone Mountain, Georgia. *Left to right,* Conrad's Encore, Ch. Conrad's Music Maestro, Conrad's Disc Jockey, Conrad's Stop The Music, and Conrad's Baby Doll. All of these Collies completed their championships. The two at the right already had points at just over six months old.

housed. A puppy is not an inanimate toy; it is a living thing with a right to be loved and handled respectfully, treatment which will reflect in the dog's attitude toward your child as both mature together. Never permit your children's playmates to mishandle the puppy, tormenting the puppy until it turns on the children in self-defense. Children often do not realize how rough is too rough. You, as a responsible adult, are obligated to assure that your puppy's relationship with children is a pleasant one.

Do not start out by spoiling your puppy. A puppy is usually pretty smart and can be quite demanding. What you had considered to be "just for tonight" may be accepted by the puppy as "for keeps." Be firm with him, strike a routine, and stick to it. The puppy will learn more quickly this way, and everyone will be happier at the result. A radio playing softly or a dim night light are often comforting to a puppy as it gets accustomed to new surroundings and should be provided in preference to bringing the puppy to bed with you—unless, of course, you intend him to share the bed as a permanent arrangement.

SOCIALIZING AND TRAINING

Socialization and training of your puppy should start the very day of his arrival in your home. Never address him without calling him by name. A short, simple name is the easiest to teach as it catches the dog's attention quickly, so avoid elaborate call names. Always address the dog by the same name, not a whole series of pet names; the latter will only confuse the puppy.

Use his name clearly and call the puppy over to you when you see him awake and wandering about. When he comes, make a big fuss over him for being such a good dog. He thus will quickly associate the sound of his name with coming to you and a pleasant happening.

Several hours after the puppy's arrival is not too soon to start accustoming him to the feel of a light collar. He may hardly notice it; or he may struggle, roll over, and try to rub it off his neck with his paws. Divert his attention when this occurs by offering a tasty snack or a toy (starting a game with him) or by petting him. Before long he will have accepted the strange feeling around his neck and no longer appear aware of it. Next comes the lead. Attach it and then immediately take the puppy outside or otherwise try to divert his attention with things to see and sniff. He may struggle against the lead at first, biting at it and trying to free himself. Do not pull him with it at this point; just hold the end loosely and try to follow him if he starts off in any direction. Normally his attention will soon turn to investigating his surroundings if he is outside or you have taken him into an unfamiliar room in your house; curiosity will take over and he will become interested in sniffing around the surroundings. Just follow him with the lead slackly held until he seems to have completely forgotten about it; then try with gentle urging to get him to follow you. Don't be rough or jerk at him; just tug gently on the lead in short quick motions (steady pulling can become a battle of wills), repeating his name or try-

Azalea Hill Deep River Leah, C.D.X. as six-week-puppy enjoying her toy. Bred by Mrs. Richmond Fairbanks and owned by Kathy V. Moll.

ing to get him to follow your hand which is holding a bit of food or an interesting toy. If you have an older lead-trained dog, then it should be a cinch to get the puppy to follow along after *him*. In any event, the average puppy learns quite quickly and will soon be trotting along nicely on the lead. Once that point has been reached, the next step is to teach him to follow on your left side, or heel. Of course this will not likely be accomplished all in one day but should be done with short training periods over the course of several days until you are satisfied with the result.

During the course of house training your puppy, you will need to take him out frequently and at regular intervals: first thing in the morning directly from the crate, immediately after meals, after the puppy has been napping, or when you notice that the puppy is looking for a spot. Choose more or less the same place to take the puppy each time so that a pattern will be established. If he does not go immediately, do not return him to the house as he will probably relieve himself the moment he is inside. Stay out with him until he has finished; then be lavish with your praise for his good behavior. If you catch the puppy having an accident indoors, grab him firmly and rush him outside, sharply saying "No!" as you pick him up. If you do not see the accident occur, there is little point in doing anything except cleaning it up, as once it has happened and been forgotten, the puppy will most likely not even realize why you are scolding him.

Especially if you live in a big city or are away many hours at a time, having a dog that is trained to go on paper has some very definite advantages. To do this, one proceeds pretty much the same way as taking the puppy outdoors, except now you place the puppy on the newspaper at the proper time. The paper should always be kept in the same spot. An easy way to paper train a puppy if you have a playpen for it or an exercise pen is to line the area with newspapers; then gradually, every day or so, remove a section of newspaper until you are down to just one or two. The puppy acquires the habit of using the paper; and as the prepared area grows smaller, in the majority of cases the dog will continue to use whatever paper is still available. It is pleasant, if the dog is alone for an excessive length of time, to be able to feel that if he needs it the paper is there and will be used.

The puppy should form the habit of spending a certain amount of time in his crate, even when you are home. Sometimes the puppy will do this voluntarily, but if not, he should be taught to do so, which is accomplished by leading the puppy over by his collar, gently pushing him inside, and saying firmly, "Down" or "Stay." Whatever expression you use to give the command, stick to the very same one each time for each act. Repetition is the big thing in training—and so is association with what the dog is expected to do. When you mean "Sit" always say exactly that. "Stay" should mean *only* that the dog should remain where he receives the command. "Down" means something else again. Do not confuse the dog by shuffling the commands, as this will create training problems for you.

As soon as he has had his immunization shots, take your puppy with you whenever and wherever possible. There is nothing that will build a self-confident, stable dog like socialization, and it is extremely important that you plan and give the time and energy necessary for this whether your dog is to be a show dog or a pleasant, well-adjusted family member. Take your puppy in the car so that he will learn to enjoy riding and not become carsick as dogs may do if they are infrequent travelers. Take him anywhere you are going where you are certain he will be welcome: visiting friends and relatives (if they do not have housepets who may resent the visit), busy shopping centers (keeping him always on lead), or just walking around the streets of your town. If someone admires him (as always seems to happen when one is out with puppies), encourage the stranger to pet and talk with him.

Royal Rock Show Time taking Winners Bitch, daughter of Erins Own Professors Touch ex Royal Rock Show Boat, at Westminster Kennel Club in 1961.

Socialization of this type brings out the best in your puppy and helps him grow up with a friendly outlook, liking the world and its inhabitants. The worst thing that can be done to a puppy's personality is to overly shelter him. By always keeping him at home away from things and people unfamiliar to him you may be creating a personality problem for the mature dog that will be a cross for you to bear later on.

FEEDING YOUR DOG

Time was when providing nourishing food for dogs involved a far more complicated procedure than people now feel is necessary. The old school of thought was that the daily ration must consist of fresh beef, vegetables, cereal, egg yolks, and cottage cheese as basics with such additions as brewer's yeast and vitamin tablets on a daily basis.

During recent years, however, many minds have changed regarding this procedure. Eggs, cottage cheese, and supplements to the diet are still given, but the basic method of feeding dogs has changed; and the change has been, in the opinion of many authorities, definitely for the better. The school of thought now is that you are doing your dogs a favor when you feed them some of the fine commerically prepared dog foods in preference to your own home-cooked concoctions.

The reason behind this new outlook is easily understandable. The dog food industry has grown to be a major one, participated in by some of the best known and most respected names in America. These trusted firms, it is agreed, turn out excellent products, so people are feeding their dog food preparations with confidence and the dogs are thriving, living longer, happier, and healthier lives than ever before. What more could one want?

There are at least half a dozen absolutely top-grade dry foods to be mixed with broth or water and served to your dog according to directions. There are all sorts of canned meats, and there are several kinds of "convenience foods," those in a packet which you open and dump out into the dog's dish. It is just that simple. The convenience foods are neat and easy to use when you are away from home, but generally speaking a dry food mixed with hot water or soup and meat is preferred. It is the opinion of many that the canned meat, with its added fortifiers, is more beneficial to the dogs than the fresh meat. However, the two can be alternated or, if you prefer and your dog does well on it, by all means use fresh ground beef. A dog enjoys changes in the meat part of his diet, which is easy with the canned food since all sorts of beef are available (chunk, ground, stewed, and so on), plus lamb, chicken, and even such concoctions as liver and egg, just plain liver flavor, and a blend of five meats.

There is also prepared food geared to every age bracket of your dog's life, from puppyhood on through old age, with special additions or modifications to make it particularly nourishing and beneficial. Previous generations never had it so good where the canine dinner is concerned, because these commercially prepared foods are tasty and geared to meeting the dog's gastronomic approval.

Additionally, contents and nutrients are clearly listed on the labels, as are careful instructions for feeding just the right amount for the size, weight, and age of each dog.

With these foods the addition of extra vitamins is not necessary, but if you prefer there are several kinds of those, too, that serve as taste treats as well as being beneficial. Your pet supplier has a full array of them.

Of course there is no reason not to cook up something for your dog if you would feel happier doing so. But it seems unnecessary when such truly satisfactory rations are available with so much less trouble and expense.

How often you feed your dog is a matter of how it works out best for you. Many owners prefer to do it once a day. It is generally agreed that two meals, each of smaller quantity, are better for the digestion and more satisfying to the dog, particularly if yours is a household member who stands around and watches preparations for the family meals. Do not overfeed. This is the shortest route to all sorts of problems. Follow directions and note carefully how your dog is looking. If your dog is overweight, cut back the quantity of food a bit. If the dog looks thin, then increase the amount. Each dog is an individual and the food intake should be adjusted to his requirements to keep him feeling and looking trim and in top condition.

From the time puppies are fully weaned until they are about twelve weeks old, they should be fed four times daily. From three months to six months of age, three meals should suffice. At six months of age the puppies can be fed two meals, and the twice daily feedings can be continued until the puppies are close to one year old, at which time feeding can be changed to once daily if desired. If you do feed just once a day, do so by early afternoon at the latest and give the dog a snack, a biscuit or two, at bedtime.

Remember that plenty of fresh water should always be available to your puppy or dog for drinking. This is of utmost importance to his health.

Ch. Merrie Oaks Chip O'Dinger, by Ch. Merrie Oaks Humdinger (sire of 20 champions) ex Ch. Merrie Oaks Black Swan (dam of 4 champions), bred and owned by Mrs. Edmund F. Mansure, La Honda, California. A great Best in Show Collie of the early to mid-1960's, with many Group wins and placements.

Chapter 12

Grooming Your Collie

GENERAL GROOMING

The rough coated Collie wears a coat that is, indeed, his crowning glory. The standard describes it as abundant except on the head and legs, the outer coat straight and harsh to the touch; the undercoat soft, furry, and dense. In other words, a "double coat."

The coat is in great abundance on the mane and frill. The face, or mask, is smooth; the forelegs smooth and well feathered to the back of the pastern, hind legs smooth below the hock joints. The hair on the tail is very profuse, and over the hips the coat should be long and bushy. Any feathering below the hocks is removed prior to entering the show ring. The texture, quantity, and the extent to which the coat "fits the dog" are, as pointed out in the standard, features of importance.

The smooth Collie's coat is short, hard, flat, of good texture, with an *abundance of undercoat*. Both of these coats will need to be groomed; but obviously the job of doing a smooth is far easier than that of a rough.

Start grooming your puppy when it is just a few months old, or even earlier. Accustom him to standing, or lying down, on a firm, steady table, lying first on one side, then being turned to the other; or just sitting quietly or standing if he prefers. Most important is to have the puppy conditioned to the fact that he *must* remain still for the grooming procedure, not fight you or constantly be slipping away. A rubber-topped grooming table, which can be equipped with a "noose" to slip around the dog's neck to steady him as you work, is an excellent investment since you will be grooming your Collie at frequent intervals, especially if he is a rough Collie. Firmness on your part will be required in the beginning, but as the dog becomes accustomed to it, he seems to enjoy the grooming procedure, usually relaxing and dozing as you proceed.

Somewhere between three and five months' age, your puppy will shed his baby coat of soft, fuzzy hair, looking quite bare for the next few months until his new undercoat and longer, mature outer coat grows in. A bristle brush is the best to use on the young puppy, and just as with a grown dog, go clear to the skin in order to assure finding any mats which may be forming. Grooming him in this manner will help get rid of the old coat and hasten the growing of the new.

The correct method of brushing a mature rough Colie, with his double coat, is to place the dog on his side on the grooming table, or whatever substitute for one you are using, and to start work at the head of the dog, parting the hair in small sections backwards as you work. It is imperative that the hair be brushed forward right from the base of the hair to the tips. Bear this in mind as you work, being careful to go all the way from the skin out. A healthy and gleaming coat is dependent on this manner of brushing, and a good quality pin brush is your most efficient tool for this job on a mature coat. You will also want a slicker brush as well for finishing touches.

If you are preparing the dog for show, it is helpful to mist the hair with a spray of water from a spray bottle while you are brushing, as this prevents breakage of hair and helps to clean as well. Continue in a leisurely manner until you have thoroughly brushed out the entire coat, spending a bit of extra time making certain that no mats are forming in the "armpits" or underneath the hindquarters. Even if your dog is not intended for the show ring, pride and pleasure are to be derived from having one's "family dog" looking at his gleaming best, and it does not take that much longer to do the job correctly than in a slipshod manner.

When you have thoroughly brushed out one side of the dog, if you've been a very long time, let him off the table to relax a few moments. If he is not becoming restless, then just turn him over and proceed with the other side.

The entire process now should be repeated with equal care and patience. When the dog is completely brushed out, let him down to shake himself; then tidy him up wherever you feel it to be necessary.

Ch. Glen Hill Dreamer's Nobleman, Best of Breed and Group 2nd at Westminster Kennel Club. Patricia Starkweather, owner, Glen Hill Collies, Middleburg, Florida.

A Collie whose coat is conscientiously cared for in this manner and on a regular basis does not generally require frequent bathing. Even if you are going to a show, you may find it sufficient just to wash his feet, legs and forechest to make them look nice and white. Of course if the dog needs it, he should be bathed, which applies to a puppy as well as a grown dog, because if he is dried carefully and kept from becoming chilled, no harm should come to a pup from having a bath any more than to a grown dog. Sometimes the dog may become involved in an unfortunate incident which may require a bath; or in certain types of muddy weather, he may just plain look grimy. But ordinarily you will be surprised at how well a conscientiously brushed coat will survive the rigors of everyday living. Incidentally, if your dog becomes

231

rain soaked, don't just let him lie around wet. Avail yourself of this opportunity to clean as well as dry him by giving him a good thorough drying with a turkish towel, or even, in emergencies, with absorbent paper towels.

When a bath does become necessary, be prepared with a rubber shampoo spray-hose, a good quality dog shampoo (many are to be found at your pet supplier's), a turkish towel or two, some castor oil, an eye dropper, and some cotton. Just prior to soaking the dog, place a drop of castor oil in each eye to prevent soap irritation, and a wad of cotton in each ear to prevent water reaching the ear canal.

Now, with your spray, thoroughly wet down the dog's coat, then apply the shampoo, lathering up briskly, working it into the coat. If the coat has become especially dirty, you may want to rinse and repeat the procedure, but ordinarily one thorough soaping is sufficient. Rinse out with extreme thoroughness and care. You do *not* want any traces of soap left on the dog to cause itching, scratching, and possibly even eventual "hot spots" as the result.

Excess water should be squeezed from the coat with your hands as much as possible, then blotted with a towel. Then the dog should be placed on a table and blown dry with an electric dryer as you brush the coat. This will turn the dog out looking his most beautiful. Of course, if you prefer, and if the dog will not become chilled in the process, you can also let him dry naturally, going over him with the brush when he is almost dry to properly re-arrange the hair. However this is really not so satisfactory in the finished result as is the "blow dry" method.

If the dog is being prepared for showing, the *only* way he should be dried is by the "blow dry" method, parting and brushing the hair as you go along. You will be thrilled with the picture of beauty he will present when you are finished!

Toenails should receive frequent care and not be allowed to overgrow, causing the feet to spread or become painful. Use a good quality nail clipper, and be careful not to cut into the "quick" (the pink vein running through each nail) as doing so will cause the nail to bleed. Should the latter occur, do not panic. Have some styptic powder handy, and apply it to the nail tip until the bleeding stops. Some owners like to run a file over the nails, either a carpenter's hand file or an electric grinder, to smooth the surface after clipping. Be careful, especially with the electric grinder (which is quite fast) not to go too deep. Any nail that has been caused to bleed should not be filed until at least a full day has elapsed.

232

Ch. Cramer's Empress Coulotte, litter sister to Ch. Glen Hill Emperor's Double Up. These are from the first litter sired by Ch. Glen Hill Full Dress. Shown finishing at Keystone Collie Club Specialty, handled by breeder Patricia Starkweather, Middleburg, Florida.

Further care of the Collie foot involves trimming out the excess hair which so heavily coated a dog is bound to grow between the toes and pads underneath the foot. This can cause irritation, infection, and other forms of discomfort, so please, for your dog's well being, keep it cleared away. Start by combing out any tangles between the pads and toes with a very fine "flea comb." You'll be surprised at the amount of hair crowding in there! With the foot turned over, use your straight shears to carefully cut out the hair between the pads, and trim around the outside edges of the foot. Comb out the hair on the topside of the foot; then with the dog standing naturally, "neaten" them by trimming around the bottom edges of the pads. Should tufts protrude, use a thinning shears for trimming those, holding the shears perpendicular to the table, pointing downward, and snipping off the stray hairs to create a compact, tidy look.

Another important area to check for your dog's good health and condition is his teeth. A tooth scraper is the tool which you should learn to use. Ask the breeder of the dog, or your veterinarian, for a demonstration of how it is done, so that you can become adept at scraping—*gently* so as not to bruise or injure the gums,—tartar from your dog's teeth.

Ears should be checked regularly when grooming and cleaned out if necessary with peroxide or alcohol on a cotton swab.

Collie owners are fortunate that theirs is a breed which requires little in the way of trimming, and this primarily for the show ring. It is of utmost importance, however, since its purpose is to enhance the dog's natural quality and assets, that it be done *correctly,* and therefore should be undertaken by an amateur only after that person has given considerable thought and study to the matter, and learned a great deal about what is correct in the breed and the characteristics of the individual dog. Thus I would suggest that you consult an expert who could be your dog's breeder, a friend who exhibits Collies, or a professional groomer in the habit of preparing Collies for the show ring, for suggestions, advice, and, if possible, to do it for you once or twice until you see how it should be done. Clipping mistakes can take a long time to mend, thus can be catastrophic if you have a lovely dog all set to go, then ruin his appearance by an error. Of course if you have several Collies at home on which to experiment, that is fine. Considering the fact that each dog is an individual and that what looks well on one dog may ruin the appearance of another, I would have an expert look at the dog (especially the head, so important in expression and general appearance) and either do it for me or show me how. In time you will learn to evaluate and do it for yourself; but as a novice, you can spare yourself anguish and disappointment if you get your dog into the ring *looking his best*. Money spent on having an expert teach you or do it for you in the beginning comes under the heading of an investment in the future.

YOUR COLLIE PUPPY'S EARS

Correct ear carriage is of utmost important in your Collie's appearance. If you plan to show him, or even if he is to be specifically a pet, you will want to have him look his best; therefore your attention should be directed to the necessity of correcting any flaws in ear carriage which in most cases can be quite simply done with care and perseverance.

Ideally, the Collie's ears are carried erectly with the upper portion, about one quarter the ear length, tipping forward. All sorts of strange things can happen during teething, including ears going prick, standing stiffly erect for their entire length or hanging low in a hound-like fashion.

Of course there are cases when nothing can be done to help the situation. But very often this is not so, and a bit of effort on your part will be well repaid by the results.

If the puppy's ears are held too stiffly erect, you will need to weight the tips forward. For this, Antiphlogistine is the product which has proven most generally successful. It is a gum-like substance packaged in a tube and available at most pharmacies. To use, first apply some lanolin ointment to the upper portion of the ear, rubbing it in well with your fingers. Then place a small dab of the Antiphlogistine to the inside of the ear tip. Apply more if necessary to bring the tip down sufficiently. Owners tell us that dogs find the Antiphlogistine delicious, so when applied it should then be covered with some protection, both against its stickiness and against other puppies being attracted to "work on" it. I am certain that your puppy's breeder can and gladly will advise you about this. In applying, start with just a tiny dab, then add to it until you have the desired effect.

Ears which hang down can sometimes be helped by trimming off some hair from the inside, edges and back of the ear. This lightens the load on the ear and enables the puppy to carry it higher.

Do ask for advice about the ears from the breeder of your puppy or a friend who has raised baby Collies. It is foolish to just let poor ear carriage remain as is with no effort made to better the situation.

Ch. Conrad's Sweet Expression winning Best in Show at a Tennessee event in 1954. Bred, owned, and handled by Roy L. Ayers, now so widely known and respected as a very popular multiple breed judge. This was the foundation bitch at Conrad Kennels, and the *first homebred bitch champion in the State of Georgia*.

Chapter 13

The Making of a Show Dog

If you have decided to become a show dog exhibitor, you have accepted a very real and very exciting challenge. The groundwork has been accomplished with the selection of your future show prospect. If you have purchased a puppy, it is assumed that you have gone through all the proper preliminaries concerning good care, which should be the same if the puppy is a pet or future show dog with a few added precautions for the latter.

GENERAL CONSIDERATIONS

Remember the importance of keeping your future winner in trim, top condition. Since you want him neither too fat nor too thin, his appetite for his proper diet should be guarded, and children and guests should not be permitted to constantly feed him "goodies." The best treat of all is a small wad of raw ground beef or a packaged dog treat. To be avoided are ice cream, cake, cookies, potato chips, and other fattening items which will cause the dog to put on weight and may additionally spoil his appetite for the proper, nourishing, well-balanced diet so essential to good health and condition.

The importance of temperament and showmanship cannot possibly be overestimated. They have put many a mediocre dog across while lack of them can ruin the career of an otherwise outstanding specimen. From the day your dog joins your family, socialize him. Keep him accustomed to being with people and to being handled by people. Encourage your friends and relatives to "go over" him as the judges will in the ring so this will not seem a strange and upsetting experience. Practice showing his "bite" (the manner in which his teeth meet) quickly and deftly. It is quite simple to slip the lips apart with your fingers, and the puppy should be willing to accept this from you or the judge without struggle. This is also true of further mouth examination when necessary. When missing teeth must be noted, again, teach the dog to permit his jaws to be opened wide and his side lips separated as judges will need to check them one or both of these ways.

Some judges prefer that the exhibitors display the dog's bite and other mouth features themselves. These are the considerate ones, who do not wish to chance the spreading of possible infection from dog to dog with their hands on each one's mouth—a courtesy particularly appreciated in these days of virus epidemics. But the old-fashioned judges still insist in doing it themselves, so the dog should be ready for either possibility.

At the Collie Club of Connecticut 1959 Specialty. Best of Breed and Best of Opposite Sex, Ch. Roanoke Rebel O'Honeybrooke, owner-handled by George W. Beaumont and Ch. Boidheach Honeysuckle, handled by William G. Myles for owner Sherry Ann Gregory. Mrs. Theodore Kusmik, Jr., presenting trophy; Stephen J. Field, judge; and Alvin W. Noble, Club President.

Ch. Arnley's Endymion, by Ch. Kinmont Chadeayne ex Ainsdale Fool's Gold, owned by Arnold L. Woolf, Miller Place, New York.

Take your future show dog with you in the car, thus accustoming him to riding so that he will not become carsick on the day of a dog show. He should associate pleasure and attention with going in the car, van, or motor home. Take him where it is crowded: downtown, to the shops, everywhere you go that dogs are permitted. Make the expeditions fun for him by frequent petting and words of praise; do not just ignore him as you go about your errands.

Do not overly shelter your future show dog. Instinctively you may want to keep him at home where he is safe from germs or danger. This can be foolish on two counts. The first reason is that a puppy kept away from other dogs builds up no natural immunity against all the things with which he will come in contact at dog shows, so it is wiser actually to keep him well up to date on all protective shots and then let him become accustomed to being among dogs and dog owners. Also, a dog who never is among strange people, in strange places, or among strange dogs, may grow up with a shyness or timidity of spirit that will cause you real problems as his show career draws near.

Kingswood Collies on the bench in the days when nearly all such events were "benched shows" i.e., entered dogs were seen not only in the rings during judging, but during show hours were displayed to the public in this manner at stated times.

Assuming that you will be handling the dog yourself, or even if he will be professionally handled, a few moments each day of dog show routine is important. Practice setting him up as you have seen the exhibitors do at the shows you've attended, and teach him to hold this position once you have him stacked to your satisfaction. Make the learning period pleasant by being firm but lavish in your praise when he responds correctly. Teach him to gait at your side at a moderate rate on a loose lead. When you have mastered the basic essentials at home, then hunt out and join a training class for future work. Training classes are sponsored by show-giving clubs in many areas, and their popularity is steadily increasing. If you have no other way of locating one, perhaps your veterinarian would know of one through some of his other clients; but if you are sufficiently aware of the dog show world to want a show dog, you will probably be personally acquainted with other people who will share information of this type with you.

Accustom your show dog to being in a crate (which you should be doing with a pet dog as well). He should relax in his crate at the shows "between times" for his own well being and safety.

MATCH SHOWS

Your show dog's initial experience in the ring should be in match show competition for several reasons. First, this type of event is intended as a learning experience for both the dog and the exhibitor. You will not feel embarrassed or out of place no matter how poorly your puppy may behave or how inept your attempts at handling may be, as you will find others there with the same type of problems. The important thing is that you get the puppy out and into a show ring where the two of you can practice together and learn the ropes.

Only on rare occasions is it necessary to make match show entries in advance, and even those with a pre-entry policy will usually accept entries at the door as well. Thus you need not plan several weeks ahead, as is the case with point shows, but can go when the mood strikes you. Also there is a vast difference in the cost, as match show entries only cost a few dollars while entry fees for

The magnificent Ch. Hi-Crest Knock On Wood owned by Joseph Reno, Carteret, New Jersey.

Kitsai's Black Diamond, born January 1961, by Am. and Can. Ch. Sandamac's Mr. Sandaman, C.D. ex Collevoy's Kit-N-Kaboodle, bred by Frances E. Whitlock. Acquired in 1963 by Edward and Milton Horton, Sandamac Kennels, Tacoma, Washington. Pictured winning an all-breed Best in Show at Dog Fanciers Ass'n of Oregon.

the point shows may be over ten dollars, an amount none of us needs to waste until we have some idea of how the puppy will behave or how much more pre-show training is needed.

Match shows very frequently are judged by professional handlers who, in addition to making the awards, are happy to help new exhibitors with comments and advice on their puppies and their presentation of them. Avail yourself of all these opportunities before heading out to the sophisticated world of the point shows.

POINT SHOWS

As previously mentioned, entries for American Kennel Club point shows must be made in advance. This must be done on an official entry blank of the show-giving club. The entry must then be filed either personally or by mail with the show superintendent or the show secretary (if the event is being run by the club members alone and a superintendent has not been hired, this information will appear on the premium list) in time to reach its destination prior to the published closing date or filling of the quota. These entries must be made carefully, must be signed by the owner of the dog or the owner's agent (your professional handler), and must be accompanied by the entry fee; otherwise they will not be accepted. Remember that it is not when the entry leaves your hands that counts but the date of arrival at its destination. If you are relying on the mails, which are not always dependable, get the entry off well before the deadline to avoid disappointment.

Ch. Coronation Powder Smoke, by Ch. Kinmont Bobbie of Borco ex Brandwyne Powdersmoke finished title in four straight shows early in the 1960's. Owned by Isabel Chamberlin, Doylestown, Pennsylvania. Frank Ashbey handling.

A dog must be entered at a dog show in the name of the actual owner at the time of the entry closing date of that specific show. If a registered dog has been acquired by a new owner, it must be entered in the name of the new owner in any show for which entries close after the date of acquirement, regardless of whether the new owner has or has not actually received the registration certificate indicating that the dog is recorded in his name. State on the entry form whether or not transfer application has been mailed to the American Kennel Club, and it goes without saying that the latter should be attended to promptly when you purchase a registered dog.

In filling out your entry blank, type, print, or write clearly, paying particular attention to the spelling of names, correct registration numbers, and so on. Also, if there is more than one variety in your breed, be sure to indicate into which category your dog is being entered.

The Puppy Class is for dogs or bitches who are six months of age and under twelve months, were whelped in the United States, and are not champions. The age of a dog shall be calculated up to and inclusive of the first day of a show. For example, the first day a dog whelped on January 1st is eligible to compete in a Puppy Class at a show is July 1st of the same year; and he may continue to compete in Puppy Classes up to and including a show on December 31st of the same year, but he is *not* eligible to compete in a Puppy Class at a show held on or after January 1st of the following year.

The Puppy Class is the first one in which you should enter your puppy. In it a certain allowance will be made for the fact that they *are* puppies, thus an immature dog or one displaying less than perfect showmanship will be less severely penalized than, for instance, would be the case in Open. It is also quite likely that others in the class will be suffering from these problems, too. When you enter a puppy, be sure to check the classification with care, as some shows divide their Puppy Class into a 6-9 months old section and a 9-12 months old section.

The Novice Class is for dogs six months of age and over, whelped in the United States or Canada, who *prior to the official closing date for entries* have *not* won three first prizes in the Novice Class, any first prize at all in the Bred-by Exhibitor, American-bred, or Open Classes, or one or more points toward champion-

Can. Ch. Whitegates Sweet 'N' Lovely, by Ch. Brandwyne Destiny's Echo ex Post Riders Leading Lady, winning her second U.S.A. major in 1968. Judge, Dr. R.F. Greathouse. Alan Levine handled for owners, Dr. and Mrs. F. A. Radassao, Orangeburg, New York.

ship. The provisions for this class are confusing to many people, which is probably the reason exhibitors do not enter in it more frequently. A dog may win any number of first prizes in the Puppy Class and still retain his eligibility for Novice. He may place second, third, or fourth not only in Novice on an unlimited number of occasions but also in Bred-by-Exhibitor, American-bred and Open and still remain eligible for Novice. But he may no longer be shown in Novice when he has won three blue ribbons in that class, when he has won even one blue ribbon in either Bred-by-Exhibitor, American-bred, or Open, or when he has won a single championship point.

In determining whether or not a dog is eligible for the Novice Class, keep in mind the fact that previous wins are calculated according to the official published date for closing of entries, not by the date on which you may actually have made the entry. So if in the interim, between the time you made the entry and the official closing date, your dog makes a win causing him to become ineligible for Novice, change your class *immediately* to another for which he will be eligible, preferably either Bred-by-Exhibitor or American-bred. To do this, you must contact the show's superintendent or secretary, at first by telephone to save time and at the same time confirm it in writing. The Novice Class always seems to have the fewest entries of any class, and therefore it is a splendid "practice ground" for you and your young dog while you are getting the "feel" of being in the ring.

Bred-by-Exhibitor Class is for dogs whelped in the United States or, if individually registered in the American Kennel Club Stud Book, for dogs whelped in Canada who are six months of age or older, are not champions, and are owned wholly or in part by the person or by the spouse of the person who was the breeder or one of the breeders of record. Dogs entered in this class must be handled in the class by an owner or by a member of the immediate family of the owner. Members of an immediate family for this purpose are husband, wife, father, mother, son, daughter, brother, or sister. This is the class which is really the "breeders' showcase," and the one which breeders should enter with particular pride to show off their achievements.

The American-bred Class is for all dogs excepting champions, six months of age or older, who were whelped in the United States by reason of a mating which took place in the United States.

The Open Class is for any dog six months of age or older (this is the only restriction for this class). Dogs with championship points compete in it, dogs who are already champions are eligible to do so, dogs who are imported can be entered, and, of course, American-bred dogs compete in it. This class is, for some strange reason, the favorite of exhibitors who are "out to win." They rush to enter their pointed dogs in it, under the false impression that by doing so they assure themselves of greater attention from the judges. This really is not so, and some people feel that to enter in one of the less competitive classes, with a better chance of winning it and thus earning a second opportunity of gaining the judge's approval by returning to the ring in the Winners Class, can often be a more effective strategy.

A nostalgic picture from 1964. Ch. Stoneykirk Reflection winning Best in Show at Mason and Dixon Kennel Club, handled by Frank Ashbey for owners John and Evelyn Honig. Judge is Edwin L. Pickhardt, owner of the famed Sterling Collies.

Winning the Collie Club of America Specialty in March 1957, the memorable Ch. Jorie's Mr. G, who is owner-handled here by George G. Miltenberger.

One does not enter the Winners Class. One earns the right to compete in it by winning first prize in Puppy, Novice, Bred-by-Exhibitor, American-bred, or Open. No dog who has been defeated on the same day in one of these classes is eligible to compete for Winners, and every dog who has been a blue-ribbon winner in one of them and not defeated in another, should he have been entered in more than one class (as occasionally happens), *must* do so. Following the selection of the Winners Dog or the Winners Bitch, the dog or bitch receiving that award leaves the ring. Then the dog or bitch who placed second in that class, unless previously beaten by another dog or bitch in another class at the same show, re-enters the ring to compete against the remaining first-prize winners for Reserve. The latter award indicates that the dog or bitch selected for it is standing "in reserve" should the one who received Winners be disqualified or declared ineligible through any technicality when the awards are checked at the American Kennel Club. In that case, the one who placed Reserve is moved up to Winners, at the same time receiving the appropriate championship points.

Winners Dog and Winners Bitch are the awards which carry points toward championship with them. The points are based on the number of dogs or bitches actually in competition, and the points are scaled one through five, the latter being the greatest number available to any one dog or bitch at any one show. Three-, four-, or five-point wins are considered majors. In order to become a champion, a dog or bitch must have won two majors under two different judges, plus at least one point from a third judge, and the additional points necessary to bring the total to fifteen. When your dog has gained fifteen points as described above, a championship certificate will be issued to you, and your dog's name will be published in the champions of record list in the *Pure-bred Dogs/American Kennel Gazette,* the official publication of the American Kennel Club.

The scale of championship points for each breed is worked out by the American Kennel Club and reviewed annually, at which time the number required in competition may be either changed (raised or lowered) or remain the same. The scale of championship points for all breeds is published annually in the May issue of the *Gazette,* and the current ratings for each breed within that area are published in every show catalog.

When a dog or bitch is adjudged Best of Winners, its championship points are, for that show, compiled on the basis of which sex had the greater number of points. If there are two points in dogs and four in bitches and the dog goes Best of Winners, then *both* the dog and the bitch are awarded an equal number of points, in this case four. Should the Winners Dog or the Winners Bitch go on to win Best of Breed or Best of Variety, additional points are accorded for the additional dogs and bitches defeated by so doing, provided, of course, that there were entries specifically for Best of Breed competition or Specials, as these specific entries are generally called.

If your dog or bitch takes Best of Opposite Sex after going Winners, points are credited according to the number of the same sex defeated in both the regular classes and Specials competition. If Best of Winners is also won, then whatever additional points for each of these awards are available will be credited. Many a one- or two-point win has grown into a major in this manner.

Moving further along, should your dog win its Variety Group from the classes (in other words, if it has taken either Winners Dog or Winners Bitch), you then receive points based on the greatest number of points awarded to any member of any breed included within that Group during that show's competition. Should the day's winning also include Best in Show, the same rule of thumb applies, and your dog or bitch receives the highest number of points awarded to any other dog of any breed at that event.

Best of Breed competition consists of the Winners Dog and the Winners Bitch, who automatically compete on the strength of those

Ch. Doral Blue Dynamic winning Best in Show for owners Albert and Dorothy Krueger at Wheaton Kennel Club 1970.

250

awards, in addition to whatever dogs and bitches have been entered specifically for this class for which champions of record are eligible. Since July 1980, dogs who, according to their owner's records, have completed the requirements for a championship after the closing of entries for the show, but whose championships are unconfirmed, may be transferred from one of the regular classes to the Best of Breed competition, provided this transfer is made by the show superintendent or show secretary *prior to the start of any judging at the show.*

This has proved an extremely popular new rule, as under it a dog can finish on Saturday and then be transferred and compete as a Special on Sunday. It must be emphasized that *the change must be made prior to the start of any part of the day's judging, not for just your individual breed.*

In the United States, Best of Breed winners are entitled to compete in the Variety Group which includes them. This is not mandatory; it is a privilege which exhibitors value. (In Canada, Best of Breed winners *must* compete in the Variety Group, or they lose any points already won.) The dogs winning *first* in each of the seven Variety Groups *must* compete for Best in Show. Missing the opportunity of taking your dog in for competition in its Group is foolish as it is there where the general public is most likely to notice your breed and become interested in learning about it.

Non-regular classes are sometimes included at the all-breed shows, and they are almost invariably included at Specialty shows. These include Stud Dog Class and Brood Bitch Class, which are judged on the basis of the quality of the two offspring accompanying the sire or dam. The quality of the latter two is beside the point and should not be considered by the judge; it is the youngsters who count, and the quality of *both* are to be averaged to decide which sire or dam is the best and most consistent producer. Then there is the Brace Class (which, at all-breed shows, moves up to Best Brace in each Variety Group and then Best Brace in Show), which is judged on the similarity and evenness of appearance of the two members of the brace. In other words, the two dogs should look like identical twins in size, color, and conformation and should move together almost as a single dog, one person handling with precision and ease. The same applies to the Team Class competition, except that four dogs are involved and, if necessary, two handlers.

The Veterans Class is for the older dogs, the minimum age of whom is seven years. This class is judged on the quality of the dogs, as the

Ch. Waljon's Cisco Kid, by Ch. Parader's Bold Venture ex Ch. Waljon's Tantalizer, a winner of the early 1960s, owned by Mrs. June Christopher, Bowling Green, Ohio.

Ch. Conrad's Music Maestro, by Ch. Poplar Stop The Music ex Ch. Conrad's Sweet Expression, has 33 Bests of Variety, 23 Group placements, and an all-breed Best in Show. This famous winner of the late 1950's was owned by the popular multiple breed judge, Roy L. Ayers, Conrad Collies, Stone Mountain, Georgia.

Amber Lace of Clendon Brook is the daughter of Ch. Elegy Disco Drummer ex Clendon Brook's Mountain Mist. Bred and owned by Christine Stewart of Glens Falls, New York.

winner competes in Best of Breed competition and has, on a respectable number of occasions, been known to take that top award. So the point is *not* to pick out the oldest dog, as some judges seem to believe, but the best specimen of the breed, exactly as in the regular classes.

Then there are Sweepstakes and Futurity Stakes sponsored by many Specialty clubs, sometimes as part of their regular Specialty shows and sometimes as separate events on an entirely different occasion. The difference between the two stakes is that Sweepstakes entries usually include dogs from six to eighteen months age with entries made at the same time as the others for the show, while for a Futurity the entries are bitches nominated when bred and the individual puppies entered at or shortly following their birth.

If you already show your dog, if you plan on being an exhibitor in the future, or if you simply enjoy attending dog shows, there is a book which you will find to be an invaluable source of detailed information about all aspects of show dog competition. This book is *Successful Dog Show Exhibiting* (T.F.H. Publications, Inc.) and is available wherever the one you are reading was purchased.

JUNIOR SHOWMANSHIP COMPETITION

If there is a youngster in your family between the ages of ten and sixteen, there is no better or more rewarding hobby than becoming an active participant in Junior Showmanship. This is a marvelous activity for young people. It teaches responsibility, good sportsmanship, the fun of competition where one's own skills are the deciding factor of success, proper care of a pet, and how to socialize with other young folks. Any youngster may experience the thrill of emerging from the ring a winner and the satisfaction of a good job well done.

Entry in Junior Showmanship Classes is open to any boy or girl who is at least ten years old and under seventeen years old on the day of the

Interest in the Collies was shared by the entire Roy Ayers family. Here daughter Linda is showing Conrad's Dancing In The Dark, Winners Bitch at the Collie Club of Georgia Specialty Show some years back.

show. The Novice Junior Showmanship Class is open to youngsters who have not already won, at the time the entries close, three firsts in this class. Youngsters who have won three firsts in Novice may compete in the Open Junior Showmanship Class. Any junior handler who wins his third first-place award in Novice may participate in the Open Class at the same show, provided that the Open Class has at least one other junior handler entered and competing in it that day. The Novice and Open Classes may be divided into Junior and Senior Classes. Youngsters between the ages of ten and twelve, inclusively, are eligible for the Junior division; and youngsters between thirteen and seventeen, inclusively, are eligible for the Senior division.

Any of the foregoing classes may be separated into individual classes for boys and for girls. If such a division is made, it must be so indicated on the premium list. The premium list also indicates the prize for Best Junior Handler, if such a prize is being offered at the show. Any youngster who wins a first in any of the regular classes may enter the competition for this prize, provided the youngster has been undefeated in any other Junior Showmanship Class at that show.

Junior Showmanship Classes, unlike regular conformation classes in which the quality of the dog is judged, are judged solely on the skill and ability of the junior handling the dog. Which dog is best is not the point—it is which youngster does the best job with the dog that is under consideration. Eligibility requirements for the dog being shown in Junior Showmanship, and other detailed information, can be found in *Regulations for Junior Showmanship*, available from the American Kennel Club.

A junior who has a dog that he or she can enter in both Junior Showmanship and conformation classes has twice the opportunity for success and twice the opportunity to get into the ring and work with the dog, a combination which can lead to not only awards for expert handling but also, if the dog is of sufficient quality, for making a conformation champion.

JUNIOR HANDLERS IN THE COLLIE WORLD

Collies are one of the not too numerous breeds in the United States which have their own organization of young handlers, the Junior Collie Fanciers of America. The group was founded back in 1960 by Ann Bowley, Lydia Colee, and Mary Jane Wittger, who were quickly joined by other energetic new members.

Many young handlers have been successful with their Collies. Shelly Roos, for one, from a very early age had longed to handle some of her parents' winners, but fearing the professional competition in the breed might be too much for one so young, they insisted she remain active only in the Junior Handling competition at first. Then came the day when the Rooses had more class winners then they had people to show them. And so Shelley, then aged 12, came into her own. That day she put the first major on Champion Wickmere Reveille, and from then on, her confidence and abilities seemed to soar and an increasing number of the dogs were given to her to show. So interested and involved did she become in dog shows that when grown up she soon left the job she had taken in an office and went into a career of professional handling which she pursued for six years. Now she is involved with a career in photography and learning to develop an interest in scrimshaw, while at the same time continuing to handle, but only the Wickmere dogs. She was active in the Junior Collie Fanciers of America, helping to edit their *"Collie Jive"* newsletter, which led to her editing of the Mason-Dixon Collie Club's publication, *"Paw Prints"* for which work she has been recognized by the Dog Writers Association of America in the form of an award for Best Club Bulletin in the United States.

Noted professional handler Tom Coen was a successful junior handler, finishing several dogs during that period, then going on to a highly successful career as an outstanding Collie and Sheltie handler. His Sheltie, Champion Halstor's Peter Pumpkin, had an outstanding show record and is top producer among Working Dog sires in the United States.

Alice Burhans' daughter, Rebecca, has grown up in the dog show world, and as a little girl was active with the Belle Mount Collies and Shelties. In 1982 she had the honor of piloting the smooth Collie which she and her mother own to a place in the Westminster Working Group, the first smooth Collie ever to be so honored.

As Juniors, Dina Eilers and Sally Tabb both handled Collies to Best in Show. Many others had fine wins to their credit in their days of competing as juniors in the heat of stiff bench show competition. Since the future of any breed rests squarely on the shoulders of the younger generation, we feel that Collie fanciers can take special pleasure in the fact that theirs is a breed which has attracted so many fine young people whose talents have led and are leading to outstanding achievements.

The Junior Collie Fanciers of America is still an active organization and continues to grow steadily. A meeting is held annually at the Collie Club of America Specialty; an awards program and a yearbook have been established, *"Collie Jive"* continues publication. As for the membership scope, that now reaches around the entire United States and includes Japan.

THE COLLIE CLUB OF AMERICA HALL OF FAME

During the time when we have been working on this book, the Collie Club of America established a Hall of Fame which is dedicated to the commemoration of contributions to the American Collie heritage by men and women who have distinguished themselves in service to the breed, the club and the fancy. Inductees are selected annually by vote of members of the Collie Club of America-sponsored Quarter Century Group, which is composed of Collie Club of America members with 25 years or more of club membership.

Candidates are nominated each spring, with no living persons eligible for consideration. Nominations must be supported by approved credentials, and the Quarter Century Group members vote for their selections.

The 1983 Class of Inductees, the first to be so honored, include Albert Payson Terhune (1872-1941); James P. McCain, M.D. (1892-1957); Florence Bell Ilch (1891-1982); Oda Prescott Bennett, M.D. (1886-1944); and Edwin L. Pickhardt (1894-1969). These people were selected for this honor for the reasons which follow.

Mr. Terhune: Owner of Sunnybank Collies whose writing probably influenced more people to become breed advocates. Newspaperman, editor, radio commentator, professional boxer, American Kennel Club director. Nineteen of his 67 published books were devoted to Collies. *Lad: A Dog,* published in 1919, has been translated into more than 25 languages and serialized in countless magazines. For four years NBC carried a program by him about dogs over its radio network, which became the highest rated 15-minute show of that era. His syndicated dog anecdotes were featured in newspapers throughout the United States for more than 18 years. He died, a victim of cancer, at the age of 69 at his beloved Sunnybank, Pompton Lakes, New Jersey.

Dr. McCain: Cainbrooke Collies' owner, noted through the years as an outstanding breeder, exhibitor, writer and judge. A Howard University graduate with a Doctor of Medicine degree, he established his noted kennels in Pittsburgh, Pennsylvania. Cainbrooke Collies earned innumerable championships during the 1940's and the 1950's. His Champion Cainbrooke Clear Call held the record for more than 30 years as the outstanding dam of seven Collie champions. A leading judge throughout the United States and Canada, he was selected as one of the 20 most popular judges in America for 1948-49 and for 1950-51. His well-known thesis, *"Conservation of Puppies"* sold more than 20,000 copies. He was a director-at-large and vice-president of the Collie Club of America.

Mrs. Ilch: Her Bellhaven Collies were synonymous with Collie quality. From 1920 until the mid-1960's, this lady was responsible for breeding 133 Collie champions. Her Champion Laund Loyalty of Bellhaven is still the only Collie ever to have won a Westminster Best in Show, which honor he attained in 1929. During the late 1930's Mrs. Ilch was chosen "Woman of the Year" in sports. Her Collie Club of America Specialty winners reads like a Who's Who of Collie "greats."

Dr. Bennett, Tazewell Collies, was often referred to as the "Dean of Colliedom." His initial imports from England set the pattern of the finest available Collies, and he quickly became an international authority on the breed. His resultant Tazewell strain became famous for its homebreds as well as his imports. A member of the Illinois State Assembly and Major in the U.S. Army Medical Corps, Dr. Bennett served as Collie Club of America President in 1917. His book, *The Collie,* was first published in 1924 and revised in 1942, and is one of the foremost on the breed.

Mr. Pickhardt, Sterling Collies, was a well-known fancier, all-breed judge, writer, breeder and exhibitor. His Sterling Kennels were registered in 1914, and through carefully selective breeding the stamp of these dogs has remained in Collie strains right to the present day through Parader, Brandywine, Arrowhill and Wickmere, to name just a few. Champion Sterling Starmist, most noted of his famous dogs, produced 13 champions in years when championships were few and far between. *The Collie in America,* Mr. Pickhardt's book on the breed, was one of the most popular of its day. A National Club president, 1935-1937, Mr. Pickhardt was, until his death, constantly in demand as a judge and as a feature writer for many publications.

New inductees will be added each year to the HALL OF FAME, and the names announced at the annual meeting and banquet of the Collie Club of America. A lovely way of paying honor to the "greats" in breed history!

PRE-SHOW PREPARATIONS

Preparations of the items you will need as a dog show exhibitor should not be left until the last moment. They should be planned and arranged for at least several days in advance of the show in order for you to remain calm and relaxed as the countdown starts. The importance of the crate has been mentioned; it should be among your equipment. Of equal importance is the grooming table, which you should also have for use at home. You should take it along with you to the shows, as your dog will need last

Ch. Jadene's Breeze Along, by Ch. GinGeor Bellbrooke's Choice ex Ch. Gregshire's Little Honey Comb, bred and owned by Barbara J. Woodmancy, breeder-owner, Riverview, Florida. Here winning the Working Group at prestigious Trenton Kennel Club Dog Show, mid-1960's, under judge Phil Marsh. Handled by George E. Horn.

Ch. Honeybrook Special Agent winning the Collie Club of Greater Miami Specialty, January 1962. Owner-handled by Jose Toledo, Jr.

minute touches before entering the ring. Should you have not yet made this purchase, folding tables with rubber tops are made specifically for this purpose and can be purchased at most dog shows, where concession booths with marvelous assortments of "doggy" necessities are to be found, or at your pet supplier. You will also need a sturdy tack box (also available at the dog show concessions) in which to carry your grooming tools and equipment. The latter should include brushes, comb, scissors, nail clippers, whatever you use for last minute clean-up jobs, cotton swabs, first-aid equipment, and anything you are in the habit of using on the dog, including a leash or two of the type you prefer, some well-cooked and dried-out liver or any of the small packaged "dog treats" for use as bait in the ring, an atomizer in case you wish to dampen your dog's coat when you are preparing him for the ring, and so on. A large turkish towel to spread under the dog on the grooming table is also useful.

Take a large thermos or cooler of ice, the biggest one you can accommodate in your vehicle, for use by "man and beast." Take a jug of water (there are lightweight, inexpensive ones available at all sporting goods shops) and a water dish. If you plan to feed the dog at the show, or if you and the dog will be away from home more than one day, bring food for him from home so that he will

Merrie Oaks Worthy Son, by Ch. Merrie Oaks Humdinger ex Champion Merrie Oaks Jubilee, in April 1964. One of many outstanding Collies owned by Mrs. Edmund F. Mansure, La Honda, California.

have the type to which he is accustomed.

You may or may not have an exercise pen. While the shows do provide areas for exercise of the dogs, these are among the most likely places to have your dog come in contact with any illnesses which may be going around, and having a pen of your own for your dog's use is excellent protection. Such a pen can be used in other ways, too, such as a place other than the crate in which to put the dog to relax (that is roomier than the crate) and a place in which the dog can exercise at motels and rest stops. These pens are available at the show concession stands and come in a variety of heights and sizes. A set of "pooper scoopers" should also be part of your equipment, along with a package of plastic bags for cleaning up after your dog.

Bring along folding chairs for the members of your party, unless all of you are fond of standing, as these are almost never provided anymore by the clubs. Have your name stamped on the chairs so that there will be no doubt as to whom the chairs belong. Bring whatever you and you family enjoy for drinks or snacks in a picnic basket or cooler, as show food, in general, is expensive and usually not great. You should always have a pair of boots, a raincoat, and a rain hat with you (they should remain permanently in your vehicle if you plan to attend shows regularly), as well as a sweater, a warm coat, and a change of shoes. A smock or big cover-up apron will assure that you remain tidy as you prepare the dog for the ring. Your overnight case should include a small sewing kit for emergency repairs, bandaids, headache and indigestion remedies, and any personal products or medications you normally use.

In your car you should always carry maps of the area where you are headed and an assortment of motel directories. Generally speaking, Holiday Inns have been found to be the nicest about taking dogs. Ramadas and Howard Johnsons generally do so cheerfully (with a few exceptions). Best Western generally frowns on pets (not always, but often enough to make it necessary to find out which do). Some of the smaller chains welcome pets; the majority of privately owned motels do not.

Have everything prepared the night before the show to expedite your departure. Be sure that the dog's identification and your judging program and other show information are in your purse or briefcase. If you are taking sandwiches, have them ready. Anything that goes into the car the night before the show will be one thing less to remember in the morning. Decide upon what you will wear and have it out and ready. If there is any question in your mind about what to wear, try on the possibilities before the day of the show; don't risk feeling you may want to change when you see yourself dressed a few moments prior to departure time!

In planning your outfit, make it something simple that will not detract from your dog. Remember that a dark dog silhouettes attractively against a light background and vice-versa. Sport clothes always seem to look best at dog shows, preferably conservative in type and not overly "loud" as you do not want to detract from your dog, who should be the focus of interest at this point. What you wear on your feet is important. Many types of flooring can be hazardously slippery, as can wet grass. Make it a habit to wear rubber soles and low or flat heels in the ring for your own safety, especially if you are showing a dog that like to move out smartly.

Your final step in pre-show preparation is to leave yourself plenty of time to reach the show that morning. Traffic can get amazingly heavy as one nears the immediate area of the show, finding a parking place can be difficult, and other delays may occur. You'll be in better humor to enjoy the day if your trip to the show is not fraught with panic over fear of not arriving in time!

ENJOYING THE DOG SHOW

From the moment of your arrival at the show until after your dog has been judged, keep foremost in your mind the fact that he is your reason for being there and that he should therefore be the center of your attention. Arrive early enough to have time for those last-minute touches that can make a great difference when he enters the ring. Be sure that he has ample time to exercise and that he attends to personal matters. A dog arriving in the ring and immediately using it as an exercise pen hardly makes a favorable impression on the judge.

When you reach ringside, ask the steward for your arm-card and anchor it firmly into place on your arm. Make sure that you are where you should be when your class is called. The fact that you have picked up your arm-card does not guarantee, as some seem to think, that the judge will wait for you. The judge has a full schedule which he wishes to complete on time. Even though you may be nervous, assume an air of calm self-confidence. Remember that this is a hobby to be enjoyed, so approach it in that state of mind. The dog will do better, too, as he will be quick to reflect your attitude.

Always show your dog with an air of pride. If you make mistakes in presenting him, don't worry about it. Next time you will do better. Do not permit the presence of more experienced exhibitors to intimidate you. After all, they, too, once were newcomers.

The judging routine usually starts when the judge asks that the dogs be gaited in a circle around the ring. During this period the judge is watching each dog as it moves, noting style, topline, reach and drive, head and tail carriage, and general balance. Keep your mind and your eye on your dog, moving him at his most becoming gait and keeping your place in line without coming too close to the exhibitor ahead of you. Always keep your dog on the inside of the circle, between yourself and the judge, so that the judge's view of the dog is unobstructed.

Calmly pose the dog when requested to set up for examination. If you are at the head of the line and many dogs are in the class, go all the way to the end of the ring before starting to stack the dog, leaving sufficient space for those behind you to line theirs up as well, as requested by the judge. If you are not at the head of the line but between other exhibitors, leave sufficient space ahead of your dog for the judge to examine him. The dogs should be spaced so that the judge is able to move among them to see them from all angles. In practicing to "set up" or "stack" your dog for the judge's examination, bear in mind the importance of doing so quickly and with dexterity. The judge has a schedule to meet and only a few moments in which to evaluate each dog. You will immeasurably help yours to make a favorable impression   if you are able to "get it all together" in a minimum amount of time. Practice at home before a mirror can be a great help toward bringing this about, facing the dog so that you see him from the same side that the judge will and working to make him look right in the shortest length of time.

Listen carefully as the judge describes the manner in which the dog is to be gaited, whether it is straight down and straight back; down the ring, across, and back; or in a triangle. The latter has become the most popular pattern with the majority of judges. "In a triangle" means the dog should move down the outer side of the ring to the first corner, across that end of the ring to the second corner, and then back to the judge from the second corner, using the center of the ring in a diagonal line. Please learn to do this pattern without breaking at each corner to twirl the dog around you, a senseless maneuver that has been noticed on occasion. Judges like to see the dog in an uninterrupted triangle, as they are thus able to get a better idea of the dog's gait.

It is impossible to overemphasize that the gait at which you move your dog is tremendously important and considerable study and thought should be given to the matter. At home, have someone move the dog for you at different speeds so that you can tell which shows him off to best advantage. The most becoming action almost invariably is seen at a moderate gait, head up and topline holding. Do not gallop your dog around the ring or hurry him into a speed atypical of his breed. Nothing being rushed appears at its best; give your dog a chance to move along at his (and the breed's) natural gait. For a dog's action to be judged accurately, that dog should move with strength and power, but not excessive speed, holding a straight line as he goes to and from the judge.

As you bring the dog back to the judge, stop him a few feet away and be sure that he is standing in a becoming position. Bait him to show the judge an alert expression, using whatever tasty morsel he has been trained to expect for this purpose or, if that works better for you, use a small squeak-toy in your hand. A reminder, please, to those using liver or treats. Take them with you when you leave the ring. Do not just drop them on the ground where they will be found by another dog.

When the awards have been made, accept yours graciously, no matter how you actually may feel about it. What's done is done, and arguing with a judge or stomping out of the ring is useless and a reflection on your sportsmanship. Be courteous, congratulate the winner if your dog was defeated, and try not to show your disappointment. By the same token, please be a gracious winner; this, surprisingly, sometimes seems to be still more difficult.

Candray Woodwind's Sprinkles, C.D.X., by Ch. Candray Concorde ex Ch. Hi Vu Silver Siren, displaying beautiful form in taking one of the jumps. Bred by Jan and George Wanamaker and owned by Bernice K. Terry.

Chapter 14

Your Collie and Obedience

For its own protection and safety, every dog should be taught, at the very least, to recognize and obey the commands "Come," "Heel," "Down," "Sit," and "Stay." Doing so at some time might save the dog's life and in less extreme circumstances will certainly make him a better behaved, more pleasant member of society. If you are patient and enjoy working with your dog, study some of the excellent books available on the subject of obedience and then teach your canine friend these basic manners. If you need the stimulus of working with a group, find out where obedience training classes are held (usually your veterinarian, your dog's breeder, or a dog-owning friend can tell you) and you and your dog can join up. Alternatively, you could let someone else do the training by sending the dog to class, but this is not very rewarding because you lose the opportunity of working with your dog and the pleasure of the rapport thus established.

If you are going to do it yourself, there are some basic rules which you should follow. You must remain calm and confident in attitude. Never lose your temper and frighten or punish your dog unjustly. Be quick and lavish with praise each time a command is correctly followed. Make it fun for the dog and he will be eager to please you by responding correctly. Repetition is the keynote, but it should not be continued without recess to the point of tedium. Limit the training sessions to ten- or fifteen-minute periods at a time.

Formal obedience training can be followed, and very frequently is, by entering the dog in obedience competition to work toward an obedience degree, or several of them, depending on the dog's aptitude and your own enjoyment. Obedience trials are held in conjunction with the majority of all-breed conformation dog shows, with Specialty shows, and frequently as separate Specialty events. If you are working alone with your dog, a list of trial dates might be obtained from your dog's veterinarian, your dog's breeder, or a dog-owning friend; the AKC *Gazette* lists shows and trials to be scheduled in the coming months; and if you are a member of a training class, you will find the information readily available.

The goals for which one works in the formal AKC Member or Licensed Trials are the following titles: Companion Dog (C.D.), Companion Dog Excellent (C.D.X.), and Utility Dog (U.D.). These degrees are earned by receiving three "legs," or qualifying scores, at each level of competition. The degrees must be earned in order, with one completed prior to starting work on the next. For example, a dog must have earned C.D. prior to starting work on C.D.X.; then C.D.X. must be completed before U.D. work begins. The ultimate title attainable in obedience work is Obedience Trial Champion (O.T.Ch.).

When you see the letters C.D. following a dog's name, you will know that this dog has satisfactorily completed the following exercises: heel on leash and figure eight, heel free, stand for examination, recall, long sit, and long down. C.D.X. means that tests have been passed on all of those just mentioned plus heel free and figure eight, drop on recall, retrieve on flat, retrieve over high jump, broad jump, long sit, and long down. U.D. indicates that the dog has additionally passed tests in scent discrimination (leather article), scent discrimination (metal article), signal exercise, directed retrieve, directed jumping, and group stand for examination. The letters O.T.Ch. are the abbreviation for the only obedience title which precedes rather than follows a dog's name. To gain an obedience trial championship, a dog who already holds a Utility Dog degree must win a total of one hundred points and must win three firsts, under three different judges, in Utility and Open B Classes.

There is also a Tracking Dog title (T.D.) which can be earned at tracking trials. In order to pass the tracking tests the dog must follow the trail of a stranger along a path on which the trail was laid between

Ch. Hi Vu Preamble of Woodwind, C.D.X., bred by Mary Hutchinson, owned by Bernice Terry. Collies are splendid obedience dogs, performing with ease and beauty.

thirty minutes and two hours previously. Along this track there must be more than two right-angle turns, at least two of which are well out in the open where no fences or other boundaries exist for the guidance of the dog or the handler. The dog wears a harness and is connected to the handler by a lead twenty to forty feet in length. Inconspicuously dropped at the end of the track is an article to be retrieved, usually a glove or wallet, which the dog is expected to locate and the handler to pick up. The letters T.D.X. are the abbreviation for Tracking Dog Excellent, a more difficult version of the Tracking Dog test with a longer track and more turns to be worked through.

Ch. Shamont Sand Castles, C.D., born 1974, by Ch. Bay Mar's Coming Attraction ex Ch. Shamont Sabrina. Bred by Linda C. Sanders. Owned by Margaret and James C. Vohr, Mariner Kennels, Northfield, Massachusetts.

SOME DISTINGUISHED OBEDIENCE COLLIES

Many Collies have distinguished themselves in the world of obedience, as you will note in reading our kennel stories and keeping abreast of what takes place within the breed. A few come in for special attention, however, such as the one who was first to win the title of Obedience Trial Champion when it was created, during 1978, by the American Kennel Club.

In the case of Collies, the first to win the O.T. Champion title was Champion and Obedience Trial Champion Shoreham Dubious Delight, U.D.T., who was owned and trained by Jennifer Julander in California, a tri-color son of Champion Shane MacDuff of Koani from Shoreham Enchantee, C.D.

Second Collie Obedience Trial Champion was O.T. Champion Walstone Impulse, U.D.T., a son of Champion Wickmere Chimney Sweep from Walstone Woodmouse, owned and trained by Madeline Loos of New Jersey.

Third was Champion and Obedience Trial Champion North Country Wildfire, son of Champion Alteza Aureate and North Country Winsome, owned and trained by Sandra Hall, who lives in Minnesota.

The first Collie to win a Companion Dog title in the United States was Goldie of Oakwood, owned and trained by Helen Sullivan of Los Angeles, who did so in 1937.

Two years later the first Companion Dog Excellent was crowned: Buster Whiteson from Jackson Heights, New York.

Then in 1945 the first to earn a Tracking Title was Sirius Sirangus.

Lockaber Ladbuck was the first Collie to earn *all* of the obedience degrees available from the American Kennel Club at the time.

Many people interested in conformation competition also enjoy obedience and take pride in gaining these titles with their show dogs as well as honors for their beauty. Mrs. William H. Long, Jr., was among the earliest of these, and in 1939 Champion Master Lukeo of Noranda added a C.D.X. title, the first show champion of the breed to do so!

The first champion Collie of either variety to earn the Utility Obedience degree was a smooth dog, Champion Shamrock Smooth Rocket, U.D., by Shamrock Smooth Stream ex Shamrock Bee. Rocket was an extremely notable dog in that in addition to the honors he himself earned, he produced two champions, four C.D. Collies, and eight graduate guide dogs for the blind, plus four dogs with special training for working with retarded or blind children. Smooth Rocket was bred by Dr. Lee Ford and handled to his degree in 1963 by Miss Gail F. Thompson of Yonkers, New York.

Shamrock smooths have made their presence strongly felt in the Collie world for the marvelous working talents of their dogs. Their owner, Dr. Ford, lives in Parkland, Washington, where she raises her Collies as stock dogs. More than 60 degrees were won by these Collies within a six-year span of time. Eighteen became bench champions, among these one with a blind handler. Thirty-three became graduate guide dogs for the blind. Nine to work with blind children, and others for guiding the retarded. Quite a testi-

Bellhaven Braw Escort, C.D., by Ch. Bellhaven Enchanter's Elect ex Bellhaven Enchanting II, born March 15, 1959. Breeder, Mrs. Florence B. Ilch.

Parader's Paragon Patrician 11 months old at photo. This Collie Ch. Parader's Bold Venture ex Parader's Red Lass (daughter of Ch. Arrowhill Oklahoma Redman) was bred by Steve Field.

monial to the temperament, intelligence and reliability of these marvelous smooth Collies!

Also deserving of special mention is American and Canadian Champion Hollyjan's Hawkeye of Markay, American U.D.T., Canadian C.D.X. and T.D. Completing all these degrees at less than two years of age, he is believed to be the youngest Champion U.D.T. of any breed. Hawkeye is also the recipient of many High in Trial awards. Hawkeye's owner is Janet Holland Thomason, whose other distinguished Collies include the second smooth to win a Tracking Degree, Canadian Champion Hollyjan's Megan of Markay, American and Canadian, C.D., American and Canadian T.D.

Am. and Can. Ch. Glen Hill Full Dress, one of the most influential Collie sires of modern times, owned by Patricia Starkweather, Glen Hill, Middleburg, Florida.

Chapter 15

Breeding Your Collie

An earlier chapter discussed selection of a bitch you plan to use for breeding. In making this important purchase, you will be choosing a bitch who you hope will become the foundation of your kennel. Thus she must be of the finest producing bloodlines, excellent in temperament, of good type, and free of major faults or unsoundness. If you are offered a "bargain" brood bitch, be wary, as for this purchase you should not settle for less than the best and the price will be in accordance with the quality.

Conscientious breeders feel quite strongly that the only possible reason for producing puppies is the ambition to improve and uphold quality and temperament within the breed—definitely *not* because one hopes to make a quick cash profit on a mediocre litter, which never seems to work out that way in the long run and which accomplishes little beyond perhaps adding to the nation's heartbreaking number of unwanted canines. The only reason ever for breeding a litter is, with conscientious people, a desire to improve the quality of dogs in their own kennel or, as pet owners, to add to the number of dogs they themselves own with a puppy or two from their present favorites. In either case breeding should not take place unless one definitely has prospective owners for as many puppies as the litter may contain, lest you find yourself with several fast-growing young dogs and no homes in which to place them.

THE BROOD BITCH

Bitches should not be mated earlier than their second season, by which time they should be from fifteen to eighteen months old. Many breeders prefer to wait and first finish the championships of their show bitches before breeding them, as pregnancy can be a disaster to a show coat and getting the bitch back in shape again takes time. When you have decided what will be the proper time, start watching at least several months ahead for what you feel would be the perfect mate to best complement your bitch's quality and bloodlines. Subscribe to the magazines which feature your breed exclusively and to some which cover all breeds in order to familiarize yourself with outstanding stud dogs in areas other than your own for there is no necessity nowadays to limit your choice to a local dog unless you truly like him and feel that he is the most suitable. It is quite usual to ship a bitch to a stud dog a distance away, and this generally works out with no ill effects. The important thing is that you need a stud dog strong in those features where your bitch is weak or lacking, a dog whose bloodlines are compatible with hers. Compare the background of both your bitch and the stud dog under consideration, paying particular attention to the quality of the puppies from bitches with backgrounds similar to your bitch's. If the puppies have been of the type and quality you admire, then this dog would seem a sensible choice for yours, too.

Stud fees may be a few hundred dollars, sometimes even more under special situations for a particularly successful sire. It is money well spent, however. *Do not* ever breed to a dog because he is less expensive than the others unless you honestly believe that he can sire the kind of puppies who will be a credit to your kennel and your breed.

Contacting the owners of the stud dogs you find interesting will bring you pedigrees and pictures which you can then study in relation to your bitch's pedigree and conformation. Discuss your plans with other breeders who are knowledgeable (including the one who bred your own bitch). You may not always receive an entirely unbiased opinion (particularly if the person giving it also has an available stud dog), but one learns by discussion so listen to what they say, consider their opinions, and then you may be better qualified to form your own opinion.

As soon as you have made a choice, phone the owner of the stud

276

Ch. Gaylord's Flyer winning the 1957 Specialty Show of the Chesapeake Collie Club. Frank Ashbey handled for owner Dr. James H. Mangels, Jr.

Chalora Choir Boy, owned by Mrs. Hillhouse, winning at Miami in 1959. Phil Marsh handling. Alva Rosenberg was judge.

Ch. Merrie Oaks Chip O'Dinger, by Ch. Merrie Oaks Humdinger ex Ch. Merrie Oaks Black Swan, winning the Working Group at Salinas, California. Bred, owned, and handled by Mrs. Edmund F. Mansure, La Honda, California.

dog you wish to use to find out if this will be agreeable. You will be asked about the bitch's health, soundness, temperament, and freedom from serious faults. A copy of her pedigree may be requested, as might a picture of her. A discussion of her background over the telephone may be sufficient to assure the stud's owner that she is suitable for the stud dog and of type, breeding, and quality herself to produce puppies of the quality for which the dog is noted. The owner of a top-quality stud is often extremely selective in the bitches permitted to be bred to his dog, in an effort to keep the standard of his puppies high. The owner of a stud dog may require that the bitch be tested for brucellosis, which should be attended to not more than a month previous to the breeding.

Check out which airport will be most convenient for the person meeting and returning the bitch if she is to be shipped and also what airlines use that airport. You will find that the airlines are also apt to have special requirements concerning acceptance of animals for shipping. These include weather limitations and types of crates which are acceptable. The weather limits have to do with extreme heat and extreme cold at the point of destination, as some airlines will not fly dogs into temperatures above or below certain levels, fearing for their safety. The crate problem is a simple one, since, if your own crate is not suitable, most of the airlines have specially designed crates available for purchase at a fair and moderate price. It is a good plan to purchase one of these if you intend to be shipping dogs with any sort of frequency. They are made of fiberglass and are the safest type to use for shipping.

Normally you must notify the airline several days in advance to make a reservation, as they are able to accommodate only a certain number of dogs on each flight. Plan on shipping the bitch on about her eighth or ninth day of season, but be careful to avoid shipping her on a weekend when schedules often vary and freight offices are apt to be closed. Whenever you can, ship your bitch on a direct flight. Changing planes always carries a certain amount of risk of a dog being overlooked or wrongly routed at the middle stop, so avoid this danger if at all possible. The bitch must be accompanied by a health certificate which you must obtain from your veterinarian before taking her to the airport. Usually it will be necessary to have the bitch at the airport about two hours prior to flight time. Before finalizing arrangements, find out from the stud's owner at what time of day it will be most convenient to have the bitch picked up promptly upon arrival.

It is simpler if you can plan to bring the bitch to the stud dog yourself. Some people feel that the trauma of the flight may cause the bitch to not conceive; and, of course, undeniably there is a slight risk in shipping which can be avoided if you are able to drive the bitch to her destination. Be sure to leave yourself sufficient time to assure your arrival at the right time for her for breeding (normally the tenth to fourteenth day following the first signs of color); and remember that if you want the bitch bred twice, you should allow a day to elapse between the two matings. Do not expect the stud's owner to house you while you are there. Locate a nearby motel that takes dogs and make that your headquarters.

Just prior to the time your bitch is due in season, you should take her to visit your veterinarian. She should be checked for worms and should receive all the booster shots for which she is due plus one for parvovirus, unless she has had the latter shot fairly recently. The brucellosis test can also be done then, and the health certificate can be obtained for shipping if she is to travel by air. Should the bitch be at all overweight, now is the time to get the surplus off. She should be in good condition, neither underweight nor overweight, at the time of breeding.

The moment you notice the swelling of the vulva, for which you should be checking daily as the time for her season approaches, and the appearance of color, immediately contact the stud's owner and settle on the day for shipping or make the appointment for your arrival with the bitch for breeding. If you are shipping the bitch, the stud fee check should be mailed immediately, leaving ample time for it to have been received when the bitch arrives and the mating takes place. Be sure to call the airline, making her reservation at that time, too.

Do not feed the bitch within a few hours before shipping her. Be certain that she has had a drink of water and been well exercised before closing her in the crate. Several layers of newspapers, topped with some shredded newspaper, make a good bed and can be discarded when she arrives at her destination; these can be replaced with fresh newspapers for her return home. Remember that the bitch should be brought to the airport about two hours before flight time as sometimes the airlines refuse to accept late arrivals.

If you are taking your bitch by car, be certain that you will arrive at a reasonable time of day. Do not appear late in the evening. If your arrival in town is not until late, get a good night's sleep at your motel and contact the stud's owner first thing in the morning. If possible, leave children and relatives at home, as they will only be in the way and perhaps unwelcome by the stud's owner. Most stud dog owners prefer not to have any unnecessary people on hand during the actual mating.

After the breeding has taken place, if you wish to sit and visit for awhile and the stud's owner has the time, return the bitch to her crate in your car (first ascertaining, of course, that the temperature is comfortable for her and that there is proper ventilation). She should not be permitted to urinate for at least one hour fol-

Pelido Hot Chocolate, owned by Mr. G. Catalano, of Rome, Italy is by Eng. Ch. Cathanbrae Polar Moon at Pelido ex Pelido Polar Eclipse. Bred by Mr. and Mrs. P. W. Burtenshaw.

lowing the breeding. This is the time when you get the business part of the transaction attended to. Pay the stud fee, upon which you should receive your breeding certificate and, if you do not already have it, a copy of the stud dog's pedigree. The owner of the stud dog does not sign or furnish a litter registration application until the puppies have been born.

Upon your return home, you can settle down and plan in happy anticipation a wonderful litter of puppies. A word of caution! Remember that although she has been bred, your bitch is still an interesting target for all male dogs, so guard her carefully for the next week or until you are absolutely certain that her season has entirely ended. This would be no time to have any unfortunate incident with another dog.

Ch. Paraders Country Squire, bred and owned by Stephen Field, Omaha, Nebraska. A famous Collie of the 1960's. Sire of 24 Champions.

THE STUD DOG

Choosing the best stud dog to complement your bitch is often very difficult. The two principal factors to be considered should be the stud's conformation and his pedigree. Conformation is fairly obvious; you want a dog that is typical of the breed in the words of the Standard of perfection. Understanding pedigrees is a bit more subtle since the pedigree lists the ancestry of the dog and involves individuals and bloodlines with which you may not be entirely familiar.

To a novice in the breed, then, the correct interpretation of a pedigree may at first be difficult to grasp. Study the pictures and text of this book and you will find many names of important bloodlines and members of the breed. Also make an effort to discuss the various dogs behind the proposed stud with some of the more experienced breeders, starting with the breeder of your own bitch. Frequently these folks will be personally familiar with many of the dogs in question, can offer opinions of them, and may have access to additional pictures which you would benefit by seeing. It is very important that the stud's pedigree be harmonious with

282

that of the bitch you plan on breeding to him. Do not rush out and breed to the latest winner with no thought of whether or not he can produce true quality. By no means are all great show dogs great producers. It is the producing record of the dog in question and the dogs and bitches from which he has come that should be the basis on which you make your choice.

Breeding dogs is never a money-making operation. By the time you pay a stud fee, care for the bitch during pregnancy, whelp the litter, and rear the puppies through their early shots, worming, and so on, you will be fortunate to break even financially once the puppies have been sold. Your chances of doing this are greater if you are breeding for a show-quality litter which will bring you higher prices, as the pups are sold as show prospects. Therefore, your wisest investment is to use the best dog available for your bitch regardless of the cost; then you should wind up with more valuable puppies. Remember that it is equally costly to raise mediocre puppies as it is top ones, and your chances of financial return are better on the latter. To breed to the most excellent, most suitable stud dog you can find is the only sensible thing to do, and it is poor economy to quibble over the amount you are paying in a stud fee.

It will be your decision which course you decide to follow when you breed your bitch, as there are three options: linebreeding, inbreeding, and outcrossing. Each of these methods has its supporters and its detractors! Linebreeding is breeding a bitch to a dog belonging originally to the same canine family, being descended from the same ancestors, such as half-brother to half-sister, grandsire to granddaughter, niece to uncle (and vice-versa) or cousin to cousin. Inbreeding is breeding father to daughter, mother to son, or full brother to sister. Outcross breeding is breeding a dog and a bitch with no or only a few mutual ancestors.

Linebreeding is probably the safest course, and the one most likely to bring results, for the novice breeder. The more sophisticated inbreeding should be left to the experienced, longtime breeders who throughly know and understand the risks and the possibilities involved with a particular line. It is usually done in an effort to intensify some ideal feature in that strain. Outcrossing is the reverse of inbreeding, an effort to introduce improvement in a specific feature needing correction, such as a shorter back, better movement, more correct head or coat, and so on.

It is the serious breeder's ambition to develop a strain or bloodline of their own, one strong in qualities for which their dogs will become distinguished. However, it must be realized that this will involve time, patience, and at least several generations before the achievement can be claimed. The safest way to embark on this plan, as we have mentioned, is by the selection and breeding of one or two bitches, the best you can buy and from top-producing kennels. In the beginning you do *not* really have to own a stud dog. In the long run it is less expensive and sounder judgement to pay a stud fee when you are ready to breed a bitch than to purchase a stud dog and feed him all year; a stud dog does not win any popularity contests with owners of bitches to be bred until he becomes a champion, has been successfully Specialed for a while, and has been at least moderately advertised, all of which adds up to quite a healthy expenditure.

The wisest course for the inexperienced breeder just starting out in dogs is as outlined above. Keep the best bitch puppy from the first several litters. After that you may wish to consider keeping your own stud dog if there has been a particularly handsome male in one of your litters that you feel has great potential or if you know where there is one available that you are interested in, with the feeling that he would work in nicely with the breeding program on which you have embarked. By this time, with several litters already born, your eye should have developed to a point enabling you to make a wise choice, either from one of your own litters or from among dogs you have seen that appear suitable.

The greatest care should be taken in the selection of your own stud dog. He must be of true type and highest quality as he may be responsible for siring many puppies each year, and he should come from a line of excellent dogs on both sides of his pedigree which themselves are, and which are descended from, successful producers. This dog should have no glaring faults in conformation; he should be of such a quality that he can hold his own in keenest competition within his breed. He should be in good health, be virile and be a keen stud dog, a proven sire able to transmit his correct qualities to his puppies. Need one say that such a dog will be enormously expensive unless you have the good fortune to produce him in one of your own litters? To buy and use a lesser stud dog, however, is downgrading your breeding program unnecessarily since there are so many dogs fitting the description of a fine stud whose services can be used on payment of a stud fee.

You should *never* breed to an unsound dog or one with any serious

Ch. Poplar Stop The Music was the foundation male at Conrad Kennels owned by Mr. and Mrs. Roy L. Ayers, Stone Mountain, Georgia.

Ch. Merrie Oaks Humdinger owned by Mrs. Edmund F. Mansure, La Honda, California, was a tremendously important West Coast dog of the fifties.

Ch. Conrad's Music Maestro and Ch. Conrad's Dancing In The Dark "reading" about their show wins. Both bred, owned, and handled by Roy L. Ayers, Conrad Kennels, Stone Mountain, Georgia.

disqualifying faults according to the breed's Standard. Not all champions by any means pass along their best features; and by the same token, occasionally you will find a great one who can pass along his best features but never gained his championship title due to some unusual circumstances. The information you need about a stud dog is what type of puppies he has produced and with what bloodlines and whether or not he possesses the bloodlines and attributes considered characteristic of the best in your breed.

If you go out to buy a stud dog, obviously he will not be a puppy but rather a fully mature and proven male with as many of the best attributes as possible. True, he will be an expensive investment, but if

286

you choose and make his selection with care and forethought, he may well prove to be one of the best investments you have ever made.

Of course, the most exciting of all is when a young male you have decided to keep from one of your litters due to his tremendous show potential turns out to be a stud dog such as we have described. In this case he should be managed with care, for he is a valuable property that can contribute inestimably to this breed as a whole and to your own kennel specifically.

Ch. Jorie's Mr. G. owned by Mr. and Mrs. Raymond G. Sass, Louisville, Kentucky, winning Best in Show at Dayton Kennel Club, April 1959. Handled by Raymond G. Sass, Jr.

Do not permit your stud dog to be used until he is about one year old, and even then he should be bred to a mature, proven matron accustomed to breeding who will make his first experience pleasant and easy. A young dog can be put off forever by a maiden bitch who fights and resists his advances. Never allow this to happen. Always start a stud dog out with a bitch who is mature, has been bred previously, and is of even temperament. The first breeding should be performed in quiet surroundings with only you and one other person to hold the bitch. Do not make it a circus, as the experience will determine the dog's outlook about future stud work. If he does not enjoy the first experience or associates it with any unpleasantness, you may well have a problem in the future.

Your young stud must permit help with the breeding, as later there will be bitches who will not be cooperative. If right from the beginning you are there helping him and praising him, whether or not your assistance is actually needed, he will expect and accept this as a matter of course when a difficult bitch comes along.

Things to have handy before introducing your dog and the bitch are K-Y jelly (the only lubricant which should be used) and a length of gauze with which to muzzle the bitch should it be necessary to keep her from biting you or the dog. Some bitches put up a fight; others are calm. It is best to be prepared.

At the time of the breeding, the stud fee comes due, and it is expected that it will be paid promptly. Normally a return service is offered in case the bitch misses or fails to produce one live puppy. Conditions of the service are what the stud dog's owner makes them, and there are no standard rules covering this. The stud fee is paid for the act, not the result. If the bitch fails to conceive, it is customary for the owner to offer a free return service; but this is a courtesy and not to be considered a right, particularly in the case of a proven stud who is siring consistently and whose fault the failure obviously is *not*. Stud dog owners are always anxious to see their clients get good value and to have in the ring winning young stock by their dog; therefore, very few refuse to mate the second time. It is wise, however, for both parties to have the terms of the transaction clearly understood at the time of the breeding.

If the return service has been provided and the bitch has missed a second time, that is considered to be the end of the matter and the owner would be expected to pay a further fee if it is felt that the bitch should be given a third chance with the stud dog. The management of a stud

Ch. Impromptú Kudos finished title in 1974. Bred and owned by Barbara Schwartz, Hollis, New Hampshire.

dog and his visiting bitches is quite a task, and a stud fee has usually been well earned when one service has been achieved, let alone by repeated visits from the same bitch.

The accepted litter is one live puppy. It is wise to have printed a breeding certificate which the owner of the stud dog and the owner of the bitch both sign. This should list in detail the conditions of the breeding as well as the dates of the mating.

Upon occasion, arrangements other than a stud fee in cash are made for a breeding, such as the owner of the stud taking a pick-of-the-litter puppy in lieu of money. This should be clearly specified on the breeding certificate along with the terms of the age at which the stud's owner will select the puppy, whether it is to be a specific sex, or whether it is to be the pick of the entire litter.

The price of a stud fee varies according to circumstances. Usually, to prove a young stud dog, his owner will allow the first breeding to be quite inexpensive. Then, once a bitch has become pregnant by him, he becomes a "proven stud" and the fee rises accordingly for bitches that follow. The sire of championship-quality puppies will bring a stud fee of at least the purchase price of one show puppy as the accepted "rule-of-thumb." Until at least one champion by your stud dog has finished, the fee will remain equal to the price of one pet puppy. When his list of champions starts to grow, so does the amount of the stud fee. For a top-producing sire of champions, the stud fee will rise accordingly.

Almost invariably it is the bitch who comes to the stud dog for the breeding. Immediately upon having selected the stud dog you wish to use, discuss the possibility with the owner of that dog. It is the stud dog owner's prerogative to refuse to breed any bitch deemed unsuitable for this dog. Stud fee and method of payment should be stated at this time and a decision reached on whether it is to be a full cash transaction at the time of the mating or a pick-of-the-litter puppy, usually at eight weeks of age.

Ch. Abbehurst Again bred, owned, and handled by Billy Aschenbrener, Abbehurst Kennels, Sherwood, Oregon.

Ch. Fancy Hi Honeybrook Forever, owned by Capt. and Mrs. E. H. Conklin, handled by Frank Ashbey to Best in Show at Tampa Bay, January 1959.

If the owner of the stud dog must travel to an airport to meet the bitch and ship her for the flight home, an additional charge will be made for time, tolls, and gasoline based on the stud owner's proximity to the airport. The stud fee includes board for the day on the bitch's arrival through two days for breeding, with a day in between. If it is necessary that the bitch remain longer, it is very likely that additional board will be charged at the normal per-day rate for the breed.

Be sure to advise the stud's owner as soon as you know that your bitch is in season so that the stud dog will be available. This is especially important because if he is a dog being shown, he and his owner may be unavailable, owing to the dog's absence from home.

As the owner of a stud dog being offered to the public, it is essential that you have proper facilities for the care of visiting bitches. Nothing can be worse than a bitch being insecurely housed and slipping out to become lost or bred by the wrong dog. If you are taking people's valued bitches into your kennel or home, it is imperative that you provide them with comfortable, secure housing and good care while they are your responsibility.

There is no dog more valuable than the proven sire of champions, Group winners, and Best in Show dogs. Once you have such an animal, guard his reputation well and do *not* permit him to be bred to just any bitch that comes along. It takes two to make the puppies; even the most dominant stud cannot do it all himself, so never permit him to breed a bitch you consider unworthy. Remember that when the puppies arrive, it will be your stud dog who will be blamed for any lack of quality, while the bitch's shortcomings will be quickly and conveniently overlooked.

Going into the actual management of the mating is a bit superfluous here. If you have had previous experience in breeding a dog and bitch you will know how the mating is done. If you do not have such experience, you should not attempt to follow direction given in a book but should have a veterinarian, breeder friend, or handler there to help you with the first few times. You do not just turn the dog and bitch loose together and await developments, as too many things can go wrong and you may altogether miss getting the bitch bred. Someone should hold the dog and the bitch (one person each) until the "tie" is made and these two people should stay with them during the entire act.

If you get a complete tie, probably only the one mating is absolutely necessary. However, especially with a maiden bitch or one that has come a long distance for this breeding, we prefer following up with a second breeding, leaving one day in between the two matings. In this way there will be little or no chance of the bitch missing.

Once the tie has been completed and the dogs release, be certain that the male's penis goes completely back within its sheath. He should be allowed a drink of water and a short walk, and then he should be put into his crate or somewhere alone where he can settle down. Do not allow him to be with other dogs for a while as they will notice the odor of the bitch on him, and, particularly with other males present, he may become involved in a fight.

PREGNANCY, WHELPING, AND THE LITTER

Once the bitch has been bred and is back at home, remember to keep an ever watchful eye that no other males get to her until at least the twenty-second day of her season has passed. Until then, it will still be possible for an unwanted breeding to take place, which at this point would be catastrophic. Remember that she actually can have two separate litters by two different dogs, so take care.

In other ways, she should be treated normally. Controlled exercise is good, and necessary for the bitch throughout her pregnancy, tapering it off to just several short walks daily, preferably on lead, as she reaches about her seventh week. As her time grows close, be careful about her jumping or playing too roughly.

The theory that a bitch should be overstuffed with food when pregnant is a poor one. A fat bitch is never an easy whelper, so the overfeeding you consider good for her may well turn out to be a hindrance later on. During the first few weeks of pregnancy, your bitch should be fed her normal diet. At four to five weeks along, calcium should be added to her food. At seven weeks her food may be increased if she seems to crave more than she is getting, and a meal of canned milk (mixed with an equal amount of water) should be introduced. If she is fed just once a day, add another meal rather than overload her with too much at one time. If twice a day is her schedule, then a bit more food can be added to each feeding.

A week before the pups are due, your bitch should be introduced to her whelping box so that she will be accustomed to it and feel at home there when the puppies arrive. She should be encouraged to sleep there but permitted to come and go as she wishes. The box should be roomy enough for her to lie down and stretch out in but not too large, lest the pups have more room than is needed in which to roam and possibly get chilled by going too far away from their mother. Be sure that the box has a "pig rail"; this will prevent the puppies from being crushed against the sides. The room in which the box is placed, either in your home or in the kennel, should be kept at about 70 degrees Fahrenheit. In winter it may be necessary to have an infrared lamp over the whelping box, in which case be careful not to place it too low or close to the puppies.

Newspapers will become a very important commodity, so start

collecting them well in advance to have a big pile handy for the whelping box. With a litter of puppies, one never seems to have papers enough, so the higher pile to start with, the better off you will be. Other necessities for whelping time are clean, soft turkish towels, scissors, and a bottle of alcohol.

You will know that her time is very near when your bitch becomes restless, wandering in and out of her box and of the room. She may refuse food, and at that point her temperature will start to drop. She will dig at and tear up the newspapers in her box, shiver, and generally look uncomfortable. Only you should be with your bitch at this time. She does not need spectators; and several people, even though they may be family members whom she knows, hanging over her may upset her to the point where she may harm the puppies. You should remain nearby, quietly watching, not fussing or hovering; speak calmly and frequently to her to instill confidence. Eventually she will settle down in her box and begin panting; contractions will follow. Soon thereafter a puppy will start to emerge, sliding out with the contractions. The mother immediately should open the sac, sever the cord with her teeth, and then clean up the puppy. She will also eat the placenta, which you should permit. Once the puppy is cleaned, it should be placed next to the bitch unless she is showing signs of having the next one immediately. Almost at once the puppy will start looking for a nipple on which to nurse, and you should ascertain that it is able to latch on successfully.

If the puppy is a breech (*i.e.*, born feet first), you must watch carefully for it to be completely delivered as quickly as possible and for the sac to be removed quickly so that the puppy does not drown. Sometimes even a normally positioned birth will seem extremely slow in coming. Should this occur, you might take a clean towel, and as the bitch contracts, pull the puppy out, doing so gently and with utmost care. If, once the puppy is delivered, it shows little signs of life, take a rough turkish towel and massage the puppy's chest by rubbing quite briskly back and forth. Con-

Opposite page: Ch. Accalia Presidential Timber, by Ch. Accalia's Mr. Timber ex Bobbie-Jean's Chicory, in December 1969. Owned by Mr. and Mrs. John Honig, Worcester, Massachusetts.

tinue this for about fifteen minutes, and be sure that the mouth is free of liquid. It may be necessary to try mouth- to-mouth breathing, which is done by pressing the puppy's jaws open and, using a finger, depressing the tongue which may be stuck to the roof of the mouth. Then place your mouth against the puppy's and blow hard down the puppy's throat. Rub the puppy's chest with the towel again and try artificial respiration, pressing the sides of the chest together slowly and rhythmically—in and out, in and out. Keep trying one method or the other for at least twenty minutes before giving up. You may be rewarded with a live puppy who otherwise would not have made it.

If you are successful in bringing the puppy around, do not immediately put it back with the mother as it should be kept extra warm. Put it in a cardboard box on an electric heating pad or, if it is the time of year when your heat is running, near a radiator or near the fireplace or stove. As soon as the rest of the litter has been born, it then can join the others.

An hour or more may elapse between puppies, which is fine so long as the bitch seems comfortable and is neither straining nor contracting. She should not be permitted to remain unassisted for more than an hour if she does continue to contract. This is when you should get her to your veterinarian, whom you should already have alerted to the possibility of a problem existing. He should examine her and perhaps give her a shot of Pituitrin. In some cases the veterinarian may find that a Caesarean section is necessary due to a puppy being lodged in a manner making normal delivery impossible. Sometimes this is caused by an abnormally large puppy, or it may just be that the puppy is simply turned in the wrong position. If the bitch does require a Caesarean section, the puppies already born must be kept warm in their cardboard box with a heating pad under the box.

Once the section is done, get the bitch and the puppies home. Do not attempt to put the puppies in with the bitch until she has regained consciousness as she may unknowingly hurt them. But do get them back to her as soon as possible for them to start nursing.

Should the mother lack milk at this time, the puppies must be fed by hand, kept very warm, and held onto the mother's teats several times a day in order to stimulate and encourage the secretion of milk, which should start shortly.

The Rough Collie Ch. Blue Smoke of Lyn-Car winning Best in Show at Tennessee Valley Kennel Club 1963. Handled by Mrs. Donna Martin for Mrs. Sidney D. Terr, Louisville, Kentucky.

Ch. Philamours Model, owned by Mrs. Dan Eilers, wins Best in Show at Heart of America in 1968. Handled by Miss Eilers.

Assuming that there has been no problem and that the bitch has whelped naturally, you should insist that she go out to exercise, staying just long enough to make herself comfortable. She can be offered a bowl of milk and a biscuit, but then she should settle down with her family. Freshen the whelping box for her with fresh newspapers while she is taking this respite so that she and the puppies will have a clean bed.

Unless some problem arises, there is little you must do about the puppies until they become three to four weeks old. Keep the box clean and supplied with fresh newspapers the first few days, but then turkish towels should be tacked down to the bottom of the box so that the puppies will have traction as they move about.

If the bitch has difficulties with her milk supply, or if you should be so unfortunate as to lose her, then you must be prepared to either hand-feed or tube-feed the puppies if they are to survive. Tube-feeding is so much faster and easier. If the bitch is available, it is best that she continues to clean and care for the puppies in the normal manner excepting for the food supplements you will provide. If it is impossible for her to do this, then after every feeding you must gently rub each puppy's abdomen with wet cotton to make it urinate, and the rectum should be gently rubbed to open the bowels.

Newborn puppies must be fed every three to four hours around the clock. The puppies must be kept warm during this time. Have your veterinarian teach you how to tube-feed. You will find that it is really quite simple.

After a normal whelping, the bitch will require additional food to enable her to produce sufficient milk. In addition to being fed twice daily, she should be given some canned milk several times each day.

When the puppies are two weeks old, their nails should be clipped, as they are needle sharp at this age and can hurt or damage the mother's teats and stomach as the pups hold on to nurse.

Between three and four weeks of age, the puppies should begin to be weaned. Scraped beef (prepared by scraping it off slices of beef with a spoon so that none of the gristle is included) may be offered in very small quantities a couple of times daily for the first few days. Then by the third day you can mix puppy chow with warm water as directed on the package, offering it four times daily. By now the mother should be kept away from the puppies and out of the box for several hours at a time so that when they have reached five weeks of age she is left in with them only overnight. By the time the puppies are six weeks old, they should be entirely weaned and receiving only occasional visits from their mother.

Most veterinarians recommend a temporary DHL (distemper, hepatitis, leptospirosis) shot when the puppies are six weeks of age. This remains effective for about two weeks. Then at eight weeks of age, the puppies should receive the series of permanent shots for DHL protection. It is also a good idea to discuss with

Ch. Gingeor's Patent Pending, Rough Collie, winning Best of Breed at the Collie Club of Maryland Specialty Show, April 5, 1969. Philip Blevins, owner-handler.

your vet the advisability of having your puppies inoculated against the dreaded parvovirus at the same time. Each time the pups go to the vet for shots, you should bring stool samples so that they can be examined for worms. Worms go through various stages of development and may be present in a stool sample even though the sample does not test positive in every checkup. So do not neglect to keep careful watch on this.

The puppies should be fed four times daily until they are three months old. Then you can cut back to three feedings daily. By the time the puppies are six months of age, two meals daily are sufficient. Some people feed their dogs twice daily throughout their lifetime; others go to one meal daily when the puppy becomes one year of age.

The ideal age for puppies to go to their new homes is between eight and twelve weeks, although some puppies successfully adjust

Ch. Hampton My Lady's Proof, by Glen Hill Typesetter's Proof ex Squire's First Lady of Hampton. Bred, owned, and handled by Virginia Hampton, Doylestown, Pennsylvania.

These beautiful puppies were bred and are owned by Arnold Woolf. Splendid examples of the type and quality raised at Arnley Kennels.

to a new home when they are six weeks old. Be sure that they go to their new owners accompanied by a description of the diet you've been feeding them and a schedule of the shots they have already received and those they still need. These should be included with the registration application and a copy of the pedigree.

Bobbie Jeen's Pins 'N' Needles winning at Westminster in 1961 under judge Mrs. William H. Long, Jr., owner of Noranda Kennels.

Chapter 16

Traveling with Your Collie

When you travel with your dog, to shows or on vacation or wherever, remember that everyone does not share your enthusiasm or love for dogs and that those who do not, strange creatures though they seem to us, have their rights, too. These rights, on which your should not encroach, include not being disturbed, annoyed, or made uncomfortable by the presence and behavior of other people's pets. Your dog should be kept on lead in public places and should recognize and promptly obey the commands "Down," "Come," "Sit," and "Stay."

Take along his crate if you are going any distance with your dog. And keep him in it when riding in the car. A crated dog has a far better chance of escaping injury than one riding loose in the car, should an accident occur or an emergency arise. If you do permit your dog to ride loose, never allow him to hang out a window, ears blowing in the breeze. An injury to his eyes could occur in this manner. He could also become overly excited by something he sees and jump out, or he could lose his balance and fall out.

Never, ever, under any circumstances, should a dog be permitted to ride loose in the back of a pick-up truck. Some people do transport dogs in this manner, which is cruel and shocking. How easily such a dog can be thrown out of the truck by sudden jolts or an impact! Doubtless many dogs have jumped out at the sight of something exciting along the way. Some unthinking individuals tie the dog, probably not realizing that were he to jump under those circumstances, his neck would be broken, he could be dragged alongside the vehicle, or he could be hit by another vehicle. If you are for any reason taking your dog in an open-back truck, please have sufficient regard for that dog to at least provide a crate for him, and then remember that, in or out of a crate, a dog riding under the direct rays of the sun in hot weather can suffer and have his life endangered by the heat.

If you are staying at a hotel or motel with your dog, exercise him somewhere other than in the flower beds and parking lot of the property. People walking to and from their cars really are not thrilled at "stepping in something" left by your dog. Should an accident occur, pick it up with a tissue or paper towel and deposit it in a proper receptacle; do not just walk off leaving it to remain

Ch. Glen Hill Dreamers Nobleman winning the Specialty Show of the Mason-Dixon Collie Club of Greater Washington, April 1961. Frank Ashbey handling for owners Mrs. J. R. Shryock and William B. Lex, Jr.

Ch. Parader's Tinker of Clenmor taking Best of Breed at the Eastern Dog Club. Owned by R. and C. Moriarty, Wrentham, Massachusetts. Mr. Moriarty handling here at Eastern in 1959. Bred by Steve Field.

there. Usually there are grassy areas on the sides of and behind motels where dogs can be exercised. Use them rather than the more conspicuous, usually carefully tended, front areas or those close to the rooms. If you are becoming a dog show enthusiast, you will eventually need an exercise pen to take with you to the show. Exercise pens are ideal to use when staying at motels, too, as they permit you to limit the dog's roaming space and to pick up after him more easily.

Never leave your dog unattended in the room of a motel unless you are absolutely, positively certain that he will stay there quietly

Ch. Kittredge Jeanie owned by Gladys Reardon taking Best in Show at Camden County Kennel Club in 1960. John Laytham was Show Chairman and William L. Kendrick, judge.

and not damage or destroy anything. You do not want a long list of complaints from irate guests, caused by the annoying barking or whining of a lonesome dog in strange surroundings or an over-zealous watch dog barking furiously each time a footstep passes the door or he hears a sound from an adjoining room. And you certainly do not want to return to torn curtains or bedspreads, soiled rugs, or other embarrassing evidence of the fact that your dog is not really house-reliable after all.

If yours is a dog accustomed to traveling with you and you are positive that his behavior will be acceptable when left alone, that is fine. But if the slightest uncertainty exists, the wise course is to leave him in the car while you go to dinner or elsewhere; then bring him into the room when you are ready to retire for the night.

When you travel with a dog, it is often simpler to take along from home the food and water he will need rather than to buy food and look for water while you travel. In this way he will have the rations to which he is accustomed and which you know agree with him, and there will be no fear of problems due to different drinking water. Feeding on the road is quite easy now, at least for short trips, with all the splendid dry prepared foods and high-quality canned meats available. A variety of lightweight, refillable water containers can be bought at many types of stores.

Be careful always to leave sufficient openings to ventilate your car when the dog will be alone in it. Remember that during the summer, the rays of the sun can make an inferno of a closed car within only a few minutes, so leave enough window space open to provide air circulation. Again, if your dog is in a crate, this can be done quite safely. The fact that you have left the car in a shady spot is not always a guarantee that you will find conditions the same when you return. Don't forget that the position of the sun changes in a matter of minutes, and the car you left nicely shaded half an hour ago can be getting full sunlight far more quickly than you may realize. So, if you leave a dog in the car, make sure there is sufficient ventilation and check back frequently to ascertain that all is well.

If you are going to another country, you will need a health certificate from your veterinarian for each dog you are taking with you, certifying that each has had rabies shots within the required time preceding your visit.

Ainsdale Fool's Gold is by Ch. Brandwyne No Foolin' ex a daughter of Ch. Parader's Bold Venture. Owned by Ainsdale Kennels, Mrs. Sophie and Patricia Peckelis, Ainsdale Collies, Great Neck, New York.

Chapter 17

Responsibilities of Breeders and Owners

The first responsibility of any person breeding dogs is to do so with care, forethought, and deliberation. It is inexcusable to breed more litters than you need to carry on your show program or to perpetuate your bloodlines. A responsible breeder should not cause a litter to be born without definite plans for the safe and happy disposition of the puppies.

A responsible dog breeder makes absolutely certain, so far as is humanly possible, that the home to which one of his puppies will go is a good home, one that offers proper care and an enthusiastic owner. To be admired are those breeders who insist on visiting (although doing so is not always feasible) the prospective owners of their puppies to see if they have suitable facilities for keeping a dog, and to find out if they understand the responsibility involved, and if all members of the household are in accord regarding the desirability of owning one. All breeders should carefully check out the credentials of prospective purchasers to be sure that the puppy is being placed in responsible hands.

No breeder ever wants a puppy or grown dog he has raised to wind up in an animal shelter, in an experimental laboratory, or as a victim of a speeding car. While complete control of such a situation may be impossible, it is important to make every effort to turn over dogs to responsible people. When selling a puppy, it is a good idea to do so with the understanding that should it become necessary to place the

Three old people. Ch. Pelido Copper Beech with his daughter, Ch. Pelido Angel Fingers and his son Ch. Pelido Pussy Willow. All three of these lovely English champions bred and owned by Mr. and Mrs. P. W. Burtenshaw, Godalming, Surrey, England.

dog in other hands, the purchaser will first contact you, the breeder. You may want to help in some way, possibly by buying or taking back the dog or placing it elsewhere. It is not fair to just sell puppies and then never again give a thought to their welfare. Family problems arise, people may be forced to move where dogs are prohibited, or people just plain grow bored with a dog and its care. Thus the dog becomes a victim. You, as the dog's breeder, should concern yourself with the welfare of each of your dogs and see to it that the dog remains in good hands.

The final obligation every dog owner shares, be there just one dog or

Silhouette against the lake at dusk. Ch. Windarla's World Seeker in May 1984. Owner, Marlene R. Nicholson. Photo by Lynn Sanders.

an entire kennel involved, is that of making detailed, explicit plans for the future of these dearly loved animals in the event of the owner's death. Far too many people are apt to procrastinate and leave this very important matter unattended to, feeling that everything will work out or that "someone will see to them." The latter is not too likely, at least not to the benefit of the dogs, unless you have done some advance planning which will assure their future well-being.

Life is filled with the unexpected, and even the youngest, healthiest, most robust of us may be the victim of a fatal accident or sudden illness. The fate of your dogs, so entirely in your hands, should never be

Headstudy of the famous Rough Collie Ch. Shamont Stormalong owned by Mariner Kennels, Peg and Jim Vohr, Northfield, Massachusetts.

left to chance. If you have not already done so, please get together with your lawyer and set up a clause in your will specifying what you want done with each of your dogs, to whom they will be entrusted (after first making absolutely certain that the person selected is willing and able to assume the responsibility), and telling the locations of all registration papers, pedigrees, and kennel records. Just think of the possibilities which might happen otherwise! If there is another family member who shares your love of the dogs, that is good and you have less to worry about. But if your heirs are not dog-oriented, they will hardly know how to proceed or how to cope with the dogs themselves, and they may wind up disposing of or caring for your dogs in a manner that would break your heart were you around to know about it.

It is advisable to have in your will specific instructions concerning each of your dogs. A friend, also a dog person who regards her own dogs with the same concern and esteem as do we, may agree to take over their care until they can be placed accordingly and will make certain that all will work out as you have planned. This person's name and phone number can be prominently displayed in your van or car and in your wallet. Your lawyer can be made aware of this fact. This can all be spelled out in your will. The friend can have a signed check of yours to be used in case of an emergency or accident when you are travelling with the dogs; this check can be used to cover her expense to come and take over the care of your dogs should anything happen to make it impossible for you to do so. This is the least any dog owner should do in preparation for the time their dogs suddenly find themselves without them. There have been so many sad cases of dogs unprovided for by their loving owners, left to heirs who couldn't care less and who disposed of them in any way at all to get rid of them, or left to heirs who kept and neglected them under the misguided idea that they were providing them "a fine home with lots of freedom." These misfortunes must be prevented from befalling your own dogs who have meant so much to you!

Index

General Index

A

A.D. Axelander Perpetual Trophy, 62

AKC Gazette, 268

American Kennel Club (A.K.C), 23, 194, 206, 213, 243, 244, 249, 255, 271

American Kennel Club Stud Book, 24, 246

American Smooth Collie Association, 42, 47

American-bred Class, 244, 246, 248

Application form, 213

B

Baiting, 264

Bath, 232

Bed, 215

Best Brace, 251

Best in Show, 251

Best Junior Handler, 255

Best of Breed, 249, 251, 253

Best of Opposite Sex, 249

Best of Variety, 249

Best of Winners, 249

Bitch, 207

Bite, 238

Brace Class, 251

Bred-by Exhibitor Class, 244, 246, 248

Breech birth, 294

Breeding, 275-301

Brood bitch, 281

Brood Bitch Class, 251

Brucellosis, 278, 280

Brushing, 230

C

Caesarean section, 296

Care, 215-235

Collar, 218, 222

"Colley dogs," 10

Collie Club of America (C.C.A.), 23, 24, 193

Collie Club of America Hall of Fame, 257-258

Collie Five, 256, 257

Collie, in America, 23-29

Collie, in Australia, 123-128

Collie, in Canada, 103-109

Collie, in Great Britain, 16-21, 111-121

Collie, Smooth, 41-47

Collies and children, 220-221

Commands, 223, 224, 267, 303

Companion Dog (C.D.), 268

Companion Dog Excellent(C.D.X.), 268

Convenience foods, 226

Crate, 215, 216, 224, 240, 259, 262, 279, 280, 304

D

DHL shot, 299

Dog foods, 225-226

Dog show, 208-210, 210, 237-265

E

Early history, 9-21

Enjoying the dog show, 263-265

Entry blank, 244

Exercise, 216, 293, 298

F

Family dog, 207, 213

Feeding, 219, 225-227, 237, 280, 293, 298, 300, 307

Fence, 216, 217, 218

First-aid equipment, 260

Food, 219

Futurity Stakes, 251

G

Gait, 264

Grooming, 229-235

Grooming table, 259

Grooming tools, 219, 260

H

Hand feeding, 296

Health certificate, 280, 307

House training, 223-225

Hunter Trophy, 25

I

Immunization shots, 224

Inbreeding, 283

J

Judging routine, 264

Junior Handlers, 255

Index of People

Shryock, Patricia, 75
Singer, Ethel C., 45
Singer, Sam E., Jr, 45
Sleeth, Mrs. Ariel, 108
Sliwinski, Judith, 139
Smith, Lois, 96
Stansfield, Mr. W.W., 17, 21, 41
Starkweather, Mrs. D.F., 175
Starkweather, Patricia (former Shry-
  ock), 30, 75, 76, 77, 78, 79, 131,
  162, 175, 179, 183, 190, 231, 233,
  274
Stedman, Mary, 147
Stewart, Christine, 150, 166, 253
Stretch, T.H., 16
Sullivan, Helen, 271
Swedrup, Mr. I., 125
Symington, Sue, 102, 104

T

Tabb, Sally, 256
Tait, Robert, 14, 16
Taylor, Mrs. T., 114
Tehon, Candy, 91
Tehon, Dr. S. W., 204
Tehon, Rebecca L., 92, 139, 150,
  187
Tehon, Stephen W., 155
Tehon, Steve, 90, 92
Terhune, Albert Payson, 257
Terr, Sidney D., 297
Terry, Bernice, 131, 158, 266, 269
Terry, Thomas H., 24
Thomason, Janet Holland, 273
Thompson, Gail F., 272
Toledo, Jose, Jr., 260
Tomlinson, G. Dean, 12
Trainor, William J., 30

Tuttle, Sandra K., 35, 45

U

Untermeyer, Samuel, 25

V

Van Dyck, Howard, 97
Van Dyck, Willard R., 25
Van Dyck, William, 37
Van Dyck, W.R., 97
Van Schaick, Jenkins, 24
Vanstone, V.A. R., 121
Vohr, Margaret and James C., 88,
  89, 179, 187, 270, 312

W

Walker, Mrs. L., 69
Wanamaker, Jan and George, 158,
  266
Warren, Christine, 174
Webb, Arlene and Luwinda, 52, 54,
  146
Werdermann, Doris, 40
Wernsman, Mr. and Mrs. Charles
  A., 33
Wharton, Mrs. A., 69
White, Mr. W., 12
Whiteson, Buster, 271
Whitmore, Frances E., 242
Williamson, Helen, 131
Wills, Robert G., 42
Winberry, Betty C., 66
Wittger, Mary Jane, 255
Woodmancy, Barbara J., 259
Woodring, Jon, 59, 66, 134
Woolf, Arnold L., 239, 301

Y

Young, Miss D.M., 167

Z

Zeshonski, Marianne, 57

Index of Kennels